The STAR Career Workbook

The very best practices in job search today.

Congratulations... you have picked up the most updated, 2019 edition of The STAR Career Workbook!

This is the tool belt for your whole career search. You are about to get tools for planning, direction, communication, networking, interviewing, and negotiation. In this book, you work!

Get out your pencil and prepare to spend some time in here.

Now, let's get to work.

 *The STAR Career Workbook*

The STAR Career Workbook
© 2010, 2014, 2016, 2019
By Dan Medlin
Lonestar Diversified Holdings, Inc.
DBA StarHR

All Rights Reserved.

Printed in the United States of America.

Except as permitted under the United States Copyright Act of 1976, no part of this publication may be reproduced or distributed in any form or by any means, or stored in a database or retrieval system, without the prior written permission of the publisher.

The STAR Career Workbook

Table of Contents

The STAR Methodology 4
The Emotional Toll of Career Change 16
Assessing Your Values, Strengths, Virtues, and Vision 34
The STAR Communication Strategy 55
Developing a STAR Resume 70
STAR Cover Letters, References and Referrals 98
STAR Networking 117
Building Your Personal Brand 134
Social Media and Online Networking 137
Define Your Target Market and Target Employers 153
"Traditional" Job Search 159
Interviewing Best Practices 174
Closing on Your Dream Job 198
Negotiating Your Offer 200
Alternative Career Moves 207
Your Life Goes On 220
The Search Goes On 227
About the Author 233

 *The STAR Career Workbook*

The STAR Methodology
The Purpose of the STAR Career Workbook

- ✺ The STAR Career Workbook was **not** designed for your reading enjoyment, although I hope you find some memorable sayings and humor here and there.

- ✺ The STAR Career Workbook was **not** designed as a mini-novel or personal journal of mine or some composite character's career search story.

- ✺ The STAR Career Workbook **was** designed for <u>you</u> to do the **hard work** you need to do, to get on the path toward a **rewarding career**.

NOTE: Before you start writing in this workbook, which I hope you will do, make blank copies of the worksheet pages so you can update and reuse them. **However, remember that this is all copyrighted material. If a friend wants a copy please invite them to buy a very inexpensive STAR Career Workbook for themselves. THANK YOU!**

The STAR Career Workbook

The Focus of the STAR Career Search

Your talents are a gift and your career is an honor, privilege, and responsibility.

I believe that God has given each one of us certain talents and strengths for a career that will honor Him. Whether you are an accountant, a salesperson, a software engineer, or a project manager, you have talents and strengths which you inherently enjoy exercising. As you stand in awe of The One who created the universe, consider that He created you for a special purpose too. Your purpose can be worked out through your career, and in doing so, your career is an honor, privilege, and responsibility.

"I knew you before I formed you in the womb; I set you apart for me before you were born..." Jeremiah 1:5

"For I know the plans I have for you, declares the Lord, plans to prosper you and give you hope and a future." Jeremiah 29:11

You want, and should have, a <u>more</u> rewarding career!

Let's pause to identify "Rewarding". Writers will espouse the benefits of being passionate about your career. They say, "Do what you love and money won't matter!" Others will focus in on the financial-side and stress that it must meet your lifestyle budget. Finally, others will focus on doing what you do well – centering

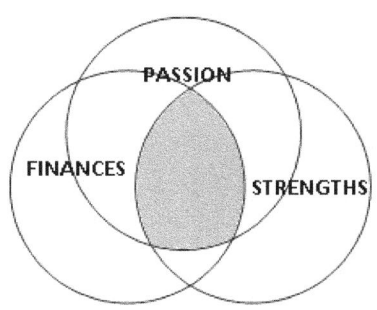

on your strengths. The truth is, a rewarding career is the intersection of all three of these factors. We are going to get you there!

 # The STAR Career Workbook

Networking to find your next move is the smartest move to make.

The STAR method is focused on networking within organizations where your passion, strengths, and financial needs can intersect. I don't focus on whether those organizations have a "job opening" that is a "fit" for you right now. In fact, I might prefer they don't, **yet.** Our focus is on establishing your name, your connections, and then your value to that organization... before they decide to fill a new position.

Your efforts can and should result in uncovering **hidden job opportunities**, positioning yourself as the organization's next new hire, and having that organization design a new job **around you** and your strengths, experiences, and successes.

 You may get **frustrated** with the run-around and people who seem too busy to talk to you. But your name and skills will be known. The team will already be comfortable with you. Your salary will not be an issue. Gaps in your resume will not be an issue. You are the eagle, perched on a branch, ready to swoop in to catch your prey.

I expect that you will also follow **traditional** paths of identifying and applying for "job openings." I just don't encourage you to spend more than half of your time doing so, and I don't encourage you to put incredible hope in that path. Regardless, this workbook will help you on that path as well.

The STAR Career Workbook

Applying for Jobs vs. Networking for New Opportunities

In the following 3 diagrams you are the STAR.

I tell people every day that they can spend their time applying for job openings, competing against the hundreds or thousands of candidates who are also applying. And you can risk your candidacy getting lost in cyberspace or summarily dropped for non-issues or assumptions about your resume content. You can even wait for the phone to ring.

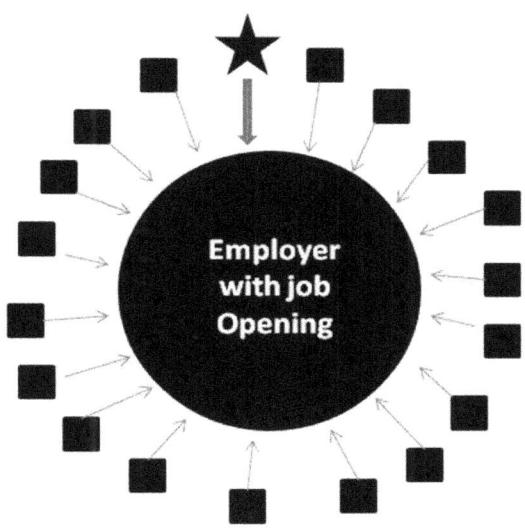

But, the Employer with a job opening is a **big black hole**. You, and everyone else, are on the outside, with no insight to the people, processes, and policies that get things done in this organization. This struggle is illustrated above.

 # The STAR Career Workbook

Or, you can spend your time picking up the phone, emailing, and connecting with decision-makers at your target companies. Investigate their most pressing needs, relate your experience and successes to those needs, and create a foothold in the organization for their next hiring opportunity. In effect, you can create a job opening or position yourself as the person for which a new job description is written, and beat the masses to the race.

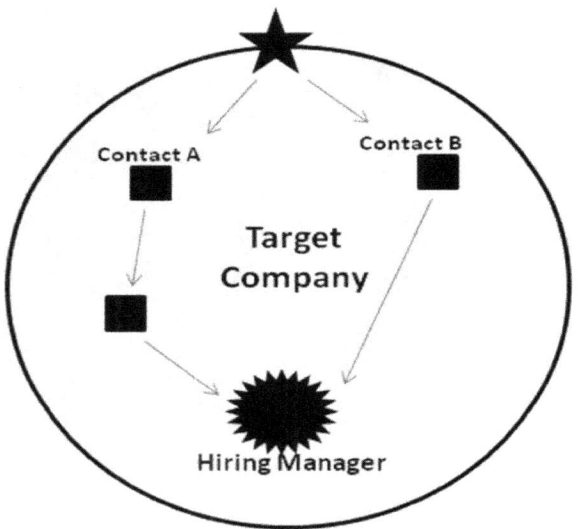

This is done through careful and strategic networking. Find contacts within your target employers, at various levels of authority. Leverage meetings, conversations and introductions until you are sitting in front of a hiring manager, interviewing for a real, open position *(or, for a job description and posting you have created together).*

In the illustration above, "Contact A" is probably a former co-worker, boss, classmate, or networking friend. "Contact B" is probably a family member, friend of a friend, another parent you met at soccer practice, a hunting buddy, or tennis partner. How you find and build these contacts is discussed in more detail in the Networking Chapter.

The reality is, often times, that when a job opening is created, the process repeats for all the people who are NOT on the inside. The job has been defined for the insider, but hundreds of other applicants are sending in their resumes with a glimmer of hope for the opportunity.

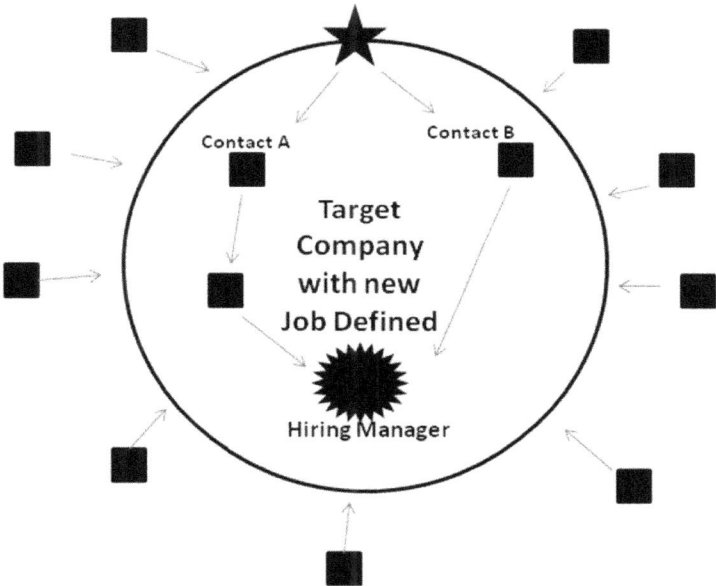

In other words, there is a strong chance that for every "job opening" to which *you* apply, there is already a candidate on the inside. Your goal is to BE that candidate on the inside, BEFORE the job is defined and posted.

Research shows time and again that teams will choose to hire someone they know and trust, over someone they do not know; even if the person they know is less qualified. That's not to say that you are less qualified, but that you must be someone who is known and trusted, so that you are the person offered the job!

 *The STAR Career Workbook*

You can also use this approach as a part of your efforts to apply for existing job openings. The hope is that you may 1) have time to establish relationships, 2) become a known and trusted resource during the company's period of "open" search, and 3) if there is some insider already in place, your relationships and your qualifications will surpass his or hers.

Note that you will often meet "gate-keepers" along the way. These are individuals who will ask you to submit your application, along with all of the other masses, and just wait for feedback. If you have contacted me in the past, while I have been in corporate HR, trying these networking methods, and if I did not previously know you well, I might have given you that same gate-keeper response. This is both part of my job and a survival mechanism. I cannot possibly network with every candidate trying to network their way into my company, but I am often the first person they find, because I am, by design, easy to find!

If there is a job posting that fits your qualifications, by all means do apply. Then reply back to that gate-keeper and say, "Thank you for your advice! I have applied to your job posting of [job title], job number [job number]. Please advise me if there is anything else I may do to network within your organization". Then continue networking and find other contacts in that company who will forward your name around.

The most rewarding job you have ever had, will be the one that you find using this method. At the end of the day, research shows that the opportunity developed through networking, identifying needs, matching one's strengths to those needs, and creating an opening for one to answer those challenges, is the most rewarding, career advancing, and potentially longest-lasting career move one can make. So, let's get to it!

The STAR Career Workbook

The Secret of the STAR Method

Let me emphasize one unique and important embedded method in the STAR program. Other career programs may use the STAR acronym as it relates to your interview technique, but in mine, the "T" stands for "Trials", as you will see later. In your STAR stories you will be asked to identify the trials (problem, challenge, or issue) which you had to overcome to succeed in each goal. This is an important feature to demonstrate your "CAN DO" attitude and your **motivation** to overcome obstacles.

There are three commonalities in STAR performers.

1. **Confidence in Skill:** STARs have the education, knowledge, training, and skills to be absolutely **GREAT** at the job you need them to do. **They know this** and believe it deeply. They have explored their strengths and can communicate why they are good at what they do. STARS are **not ego-centric** or selfish about their talent, however. Their "greatness" is graced with humility, and they are comfortable sharing their weaknesses and past failures, because they have learned from these events and improved their core strengths as a result.

2. **Can-Do Attitude:** STARs have a "can-do" attitude. They like challenges and puzzles. Everyone gets frustrated a little, when lots of variables come at them, when priorities change or are unclear, or when answers seem just out of reach. STARS know they CAN figure out a way to push through the fog and get results. A STAR may get flustered, at least at first, but most people who observe them in stressful situations will say that they are "calm, cool, and collected."

The STAR Career Workbook

3. **Passion for Craft:** STARs have *passion* for their chosen profession and their craft. They chose their career path after considering other options and have stuck with it once they knew it was their gift. They would do it for free if they could. STARs get a strong feeling of intrinsic reward from completing their work and see the long-term benefits in what they do. If you ask a STAR what they will do when they retire, they might say they don't intend to retire, or only have something in mind for much later in life. They just want to get better and better, and do more and more of what they do best.

How STARs Achieve

1. As already said, STARs believe in themselves and are confident with their skills. Again, this is not an egotistical thing. It is based on experience of both success, and lessons learned through failure.

2. Everyone faces obstacles in life, but STARs will persevere and will overcome those obstacles. There are 2 consistent laws of achievement: 1) There are ALWAYS obstacles and 2) Only those who find a way to overcome the obstacles get to their goal. STARs will be able to share examples of how they have done this in their professional life.

3. STARs succeed through pulling resources together, recruiting talent to support them, and solving the puzzles in front of them. A STAR will be able to talk about the times they were faced with limited resources and confusing scenarios, but pushed through and found solutions anyway.

The STAR Career Workbook

Motivation begins with having a strong INTERNAL LOCUS OF CONTROL. This is the extent to which YOU believe that YOU can control events that affect YOU.

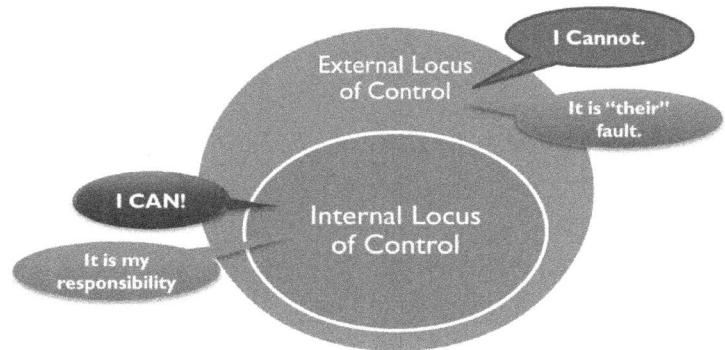

You can play the Blame-Game or you can take Ownership!

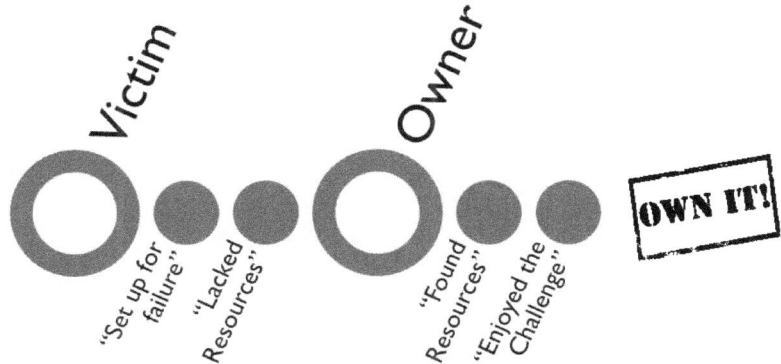

Consistently through the ages, this is the key ingredient employers are looking for, whether they say it or not. And the STAR method will help you prepare for this.

The STAR Career Workbook

Are You a STAR?

Strategic: Do you have a plan for your career? Do you understand your long-term and short-term mission, vision, values, and objectives? A STAR has done the necessary exploration to understand his/her core values, budgetary and lifestyle needs, industry trends, threats, and opportunities. And a STAR has planned accordingly. He has key objectives laid out from "having the end in mind" to understanding what 10 things need to be done today – who to call, meetings to make, branding to do, applications to send, follow-ups needed.

Trial-Tested Talent: Of course you are talented. You've had good jobs in the past and you've had some successes. But a STAR has done the necessary homework to document those successes, into concise and impactful stories, that can be told in cover letters, introductions, networking events, and interviews. Do you truly understand all of your talents? If not, let's get some exploration going about what you've accomplished, how you've positively impacted the bottom line of your employers, and how those successes translate into transferrable talents. As I've said, the STAR candidate offers something extra that other candidates do not – a special skill, a certain discipline, and ***trial-tested perseverance***.

The STAR Career Workbook

Available: You are looking for work or you are networking for your next career move. You've posted your resume online. You've attended some job club meetings or networking events in your industry. Of course you are available, right? But a STAR is much more engaged in this process. He/she is not just attending the job clubs, he/she is helping to organize them. The contacts one makes as an organizer, instead of an attender, are 4 times as powerful. A STAR is actively managing multiple online portfolios on Facebook™, Linkedin™, and Meetup™. Yet all of those profiles are consistent, each is electrifying, and all of them communicate his/her key objectives. A STAR is blogging on her industry trends, coaching other job seekers, connecting people to people, not just self to others, and a STAR is known and seen regularly at high profile networking events. Sound daunting? It is. Sound like a full time job? Yep.

Results-Focused ROI: This is the bottom line - literally.

How will you become a true resource for your next employer? A STAR is targeting employers where he can transfer in his talents, contacts, successes, and values to make a positive impact to the bottom line of that organization. What is the ROI (Return on Investment) if a specific employer hires you? If you don't know, why are you sending them your resume? In the strategic planning phase of his/her search, a STAR has identified a list of 50–100 target employers, but now he/she has identified the 3 deliverables he/she can bring to each employer that will bring them a 200% Return On Investment.

The STAR Career Workbook

The Emotional Toll of Career Change

Dealing with a major career transition, especially due to a lay-off, is extremely similar to the cycle of grief. According to Mark Gorkin, "The Stress Doc", when the dislocation from a job and a career is sudden, unexpected, and/or unwanted, there is a period of shock, fear, or rage, as well as, sadness or helplessness. You can expect, and it is perfectly natural, to experience this cycle of emotions. They do not come orderly, and you may transition from one to another, and back again. If you are caught without an outlet, in any one of these emotions, you can become stuck and unable to move forward, or you can be pulled way off track from your original career path.

The Kubler-Ross Grief Cycle Illustrated

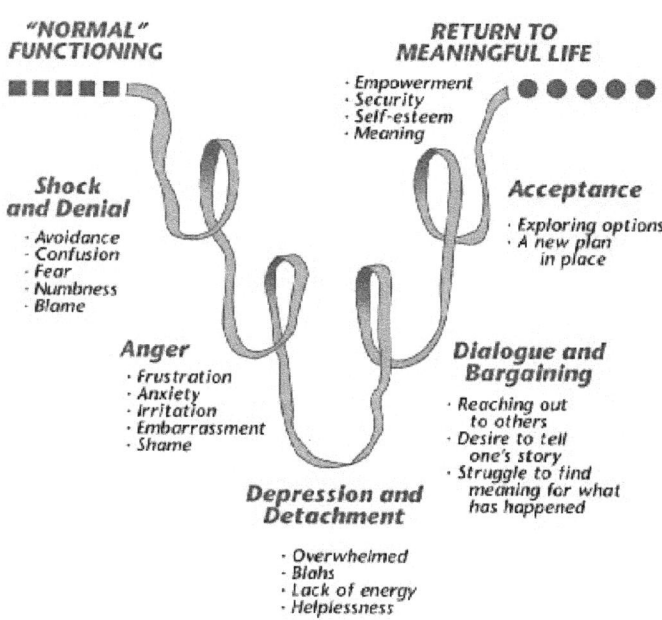

The STAR Career Workbook

Use this checklist/table to identify where you've already been, and where you are heading.

Kubler-Ross	"Americanized" version
— Shock stage: Initial paralysis at hearing the bad news. — Denial stage: Trying to avoid the inevitable. — Anger stage: Frustrated outpouring of bottled-up emotion. — Bargaining stage: Seeking in vain for a way out. — Depression stage: Final realization of the inevitable. — Testing stage: Seeking realistic solutions. — Acceptance stage: Finally finding the way forward.	— Shock and Denial or "It Can't Happen Here!" — Fear, Panic, and Shame or "Oh God, What Do I Do Now?" — Rage and/or Helplessness or "How Dare They!" or "Oh No, How Could They!" — Guilt and Ambivalence or "Damned If You Do or If You Don't!" — Focused Anger and Letting Go or "Turning a Lemon into Lemonade" — Exploration and New Identity or "Now You're Ready to 'Just Do It!'" — Acceptance or "The Glass is Half Empty <u>and</u> Half Full."

Getting stuck

A person may become stuck in denial, never moving on from the position of not accepting the inevitable future. When it happens, they still keep on denying it, for example, the person

who has lost their job still going into the city, only to sit on a park bench all day.

 ## The STAR Career Workbook

Looping cycles
Another trap is that when a person moves on to the next phase, but because they have not fully completed an earlier phase, they move backwards in cyclic loops that repeat previous emotion and actions. Thus, for example, a person that finds bargaining not to be working, may go back into anger or denial.

Roller Coaster Ride
Some refer to the experience more like a roller-coaster ride.

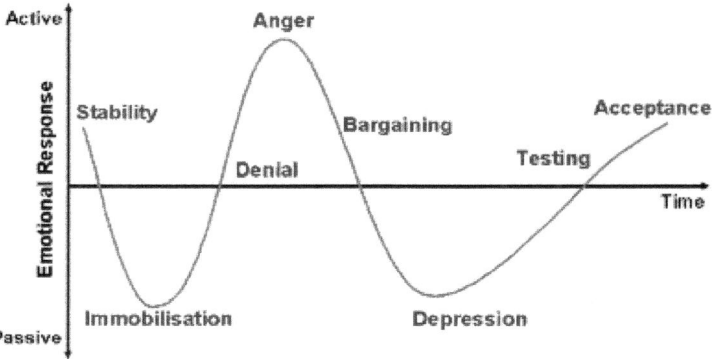

On some days you are on a high, with great hopes and dreams in front of you. On other days you are feeling depressed or angry again, set back from your goals by a disappointment or two, or you are re-living the past few months before your change, with regrets.

Other times your stomach is launched into your throat as you complete an upside-down 360! You will be thrown for a loop as you, and others, including recruiters, career contacts, hiring managers, and even friends and family, question your value, your achievements, and your choices in life. The thrill ride of dealing with a career transition is a true test of bravery.

The STAR Career Workbook

Here's the message:
All these cycles of emotion are completely normal and completely acceptable. Allow yourself to feel what you feel. Lean on your family and friends, and especially your faith, during this time of difficulty. You will be stronger on the back end of this.

Scriptures that may help; they definitely help me:
- God is close to the brokenhearted and saves those who are crushed in spirit. - Psalm 34:18
- Blessed are those who are poor in spirit, for theirs is the kingdom of heaven. - Matthew 5:3
- Be strong and courageous; do not be afraid, for God will be with you wherever you go. - Joshua 1:9
- In **all things**, God works for the good of those who love Him. - Romans 8:28

Telling Friends and Family

If you are feeling embarrassed, or you are worried about your credentials taking a hit because you were laid off or forced to make a career transition, know that you are NOT ALONE. In early 2009, the time period in which this workbook was first developed, the U.S. Department of Labor 4-Week Moving Average for Unemployment Insurance weekly claims, across the United States, was 630,500. In June 2014, initial claims for unemployment, while improving considerably since 2009-2010, still rose by 10,000 new claimants. This was over the previous averages from January to May, with 352,250 new claims for unemployment.

Looking in to 2018, while unemployment is definitely very low across most of the United States, our political system is in turmoil and companies are staying very lean, focusing on "sustainable" growth. If you've been let go, or find yourself underemployed, it is highly likely that you are joined by a number of other strongly qualified individuals, and it has nothing to do with your performance, but that it is simply an economic situation.

Regardless, you need strong allies to help you through this transition, and you need all the contacts and network outlets you can find to identify new opportunities. Telling Friends and Family is the first step in accomplishing both of these goals. **Take time NOW to think through who you need to contact and make a plan for that communication.**

1. Who, besides you, are going to be most impacted physically and/or emotionally by your career transition? They may be worried for you, worried for their own safety and security, and worried about the long-term impact of an income drop or gap in employment.

2. Each person may need a different form of communication. List some possible ways you will address the change to parents, spouse/partner, children, and friends.

3. What assurance can you give about your plans, resources, and efforts (already), to move forward in your career? (i.e. you have started using this workbook! What other steps have you already taken?)

The STAR Career Workbook

Moving Forward

Most professionals in the field of psychology and counseling, ***including me***, will recommend the following treatments to move you forward through the cycle of grief, and back toward "normal functioning" and a "meaningful life."

- **Seek support** of friends, family, and professionals: You will need safe outlets for the expression of your fear, anger, and sadness. Usually this is best found with close friends and family, and possibly with professionals trained in the field. As for professionals, seek out confidential sources to voice your pains; primarily counselors and therapists. Unfortunately, the loyalty of your source can often be traced by the paycheck. If you, your church, or the state is sustaining them, they should be trusted. If a potential employer is paying them, keep your guard up. As you move forward to seek new career opportunities, you do not want these negative emotions to spill over into conversations with career contacts, recruiters, and hiring managers.

- **Look for realistic things you can do** – <u>now</u> – to change your situation: You've made a good start by reading through this workbook. Take the next step and complete the worksheets and assignments!

- **Try different solutions**: Explore your options and test the waters on different approaches. This workbook will discuss networking, traditional job search, contracting and temporary work, survival jobs, and starting your own business. Each of these approaches can be tested. Small steps in trying them out can rejuvenate you and give you new revelations.

The STAR Career Workbook

You will know when you are not stuck, and when you are moving out of the cycle, when you are:
- Actively involved in moving on
- Actively seeking new opportunities
- Taking ownership both for yourself and for your actions
- Planning, acting on your plan, taking note of the results, and then changing your plans and actions in response
- Increasingly happier and more content

Above all, it is important to move forward now in your career transition. You will continue to feel the cycle of emotions, and you may feel stuck from time to time, but taking steps forward in your search is critical in this competitive marketplace.

Release the negative emotions safely and keep the positive energy flowing into your STAR Career.

After the next exercise, you will work through a section on what to say about your previous employer. This is often where negative energy may be directed. The only safe ears to release this on are family and friends.

Do not release your frustrations with recruiters, people you meet at professional networking events, or people you meet at job fairs.

As it says in Philippians 4:8, whatever is true, whatever is honorable, whatever is right, whatever is pure, whatever is lovely, whatever is of good repute, if there is any excellence, and if anything is worthy of praise, dwell on these things.

The STAR Career Workbook

Moving Forward Worksheet

Take some time NOW to take notes on where you are now with your emotional state, what actions you have taken to move forward, and what you need to do to move through this cycle:

1. Where would you place yourself now in the cycle of grief? Why?

2. What actions have you taken to move forward? (See the suggestions on the previous page)

3. What do you need to do to either get "unstuck" or push on through toward the stages of testing, exploring, and accepting?

The STAR Career Workbook

What do you say about your past employer?

Here is some general guidance, in addition to a worksheet to plan your specific responses.

No Bad-Mouthing: It is critical that nothing in your public statements about your past job, employer, manager(s), or co-workers comes across as bad-mouthing. There is always something positive you can say about a past job; something you learned, connections you made, and especially your accomplishments (despite the barriers).

Lean on your **personal support** network to voice and exhale the bad energy and bad experiences you may have had with past employers, and keep those discussions away from recruiters, job contacts, and hiring managers. They WILL ask you, and some will even prod, poke, and push to find out, if you have negative things to say about your last boss. Resist!

Know that **future employers are "listening"** to see if you will speak poorly of a past employer. In their mind, your willingness to speak poorly of a past employer is an indication of your willingness to speak poorly of them someday, and it will ruin your chances of a successful interview. Watch what you say out loud to recruiters, and to people you meet at networking events. And don't forget to watch what you write in your social media posts!

Exit and move forward: In the chapter on Communication Strategy, I will discuss the development of your exit and moving forward statement. Carry these thoughts forward... as you develop that script. Stay "on message" with positive language.

The STAR Career Workbook

Take some time NOW to answer these questions. Think of something *positive* you can say in response to each question. You will channel some of these thoughts later into your "Moving Forward Statement".

1. Tell me about working at XYZ company (what were some highlights, how did you create some successes?)

2. What was your last manager like? (what did you learn from your manager?)

3. What kind of future do you think your last employer has? (what do they do well, in their niche in the market?)

# The STAR Career Workbook

If you are still working, managing the risk

Companies are always looking for every cost-saving measure they can find. That includes letting go of employees who have become disengaged. While you are trying to build new bridges, make sure you don't burn the one you are on.

Stay valuable: Focus on results you can deliver in your current role. Seek ways you can help the bottom line of the organization, with new sources of revenue, cost-saving measures, new efficiencies, ability to do more and multi-task, etc.

- *What is one thing you can do this week/month to help the "bottom line" at your current employer?*

Do your best every day: Keep your productivity high. Plan your day well and execute your plan. Stay off of entertainment-focused social media sites, and do your online shopping on your own time.

- *What are some things you need to clean up in your daily work (distractions, time-wasters, etc.?)*

 *The STAR Career Workbook*

Honor your current employer: Continue to speak highly of your current employer, learn the marketing messages the company is advocating, and repeat them publicly. Recommend your company through all of your networking channels.

- *What are the short-term goals and long-term values of your current employer?*

Finish strong and document your methods for those that will follow you: As you quietly bring to a close your work at your current employer, give more than you've ever given in your passion and commitment, and then make sure your success can be repeated by others who might succeed you.

- *What do you need to wrap up and document, to leave behind a strong legacy when you depart?*

Keep your search confidential: It is critical that you not discuss your desire to move on with anyone at your current employer, even with your closest work friends. In some cases, you simply should not trust the confidence of anyone you work with, but even if you believe that you can trust them, telling them about your plans can put them in a compromising position.

- *Who can you talk to about your ideas and plans, outside of your current work colleagues?*

- *Think through your list of friends, family, and past co-workers. Who might you lean on for emotional support?*

- *What can you share with each of them?*

- *What answers do you want from each of them?*

The STAR Career Workbook

Barriers to Launching and Continuing your Career Transition

Decisions
Often the toughest part of launching a search is deciding on your direction. This workbook should help, but you will have some tough decisions to make. Know this, you can pursue multiple paths (probably no more than 3) and you can change your course. Rely on your friends, family, and professional support to get you over the decision-hump, chart and start your course.

Distractions
Once you do start your course, you will undoubtedly be tempted by many attractive offers that are off the paths you have chosen. Consider them, maybe, but after analyzing these options against what you have discovered through this work, if they do not match your values, strengths, past successes, and vision for your future, eliminate them quickly and do not look back.

Planning
Career Transition requires consistent planning. If planning has been a weakness for you, then take time NOW to learn the basics and start practicing it. Practice planning small things first: your calendar, your goals for the day, some short term objectives. See what works for you and build on those experiences. Remember, "Plans are of little importance, but **planning** is essential." -- Winston Churchill

Goals
Goals can become a barrier when a) you don't set them; b) you don't track them; c) they are unrealistic in the scheme of your capabilities; or d) they are out of line with your career path.

The STAR Career Workbook

Consistent with the STAR theme, I have developed a STAR acronym to consider if you've got a good goal.

Strategic: Consistent with your vision and broad enough to adapt to your changing environment.

Trackable: Have some form of measurement or metric so that you know when you've attained the goal.

Accountable: Determine who (probably you, but others may be involved also), how, and when, so you can identify where breakdowns may occur.

Realistic: It's good to have big dreams, and casting your vision is an empowering exercise. However, setting STAR goals involves realistic, attainable objectives, within your ability, scope of your financial resources, and attainable in the time you have available.

Family

If you have a family, you probably feel like I do: they come first. The temptation during your career transition is to put their needs before your work in **finding work**. I loved pushing my daughter on her swing and playing with my son, but those activities had to be balanced with the time I had planned to devote to my career search that day. If I took a break at 3pm to play with the kids, I had to make it up after they went to bed.

Time

Career Transition is a full-time job. If you are unemployed, you should be devoting 8 hours a day and 40 hours a week to the effort. See my section "Balance your Time" at the beginning of the chapter "Your Life Goes On". Many demands for your time will begin to surface. Now that you have all of this "free time" you, your friends, and your family will find projects, activities, and distractions. Stick to your "work week" and keep using your calendar or planner.

For other ideas on scheduling your week around key metrics, refer to the **Career Search Productivity Tracker** in my "Networking" chapter.

Money

Career Transition will often require some investment of resources. If you have had an issue in the past with managing your finances, and you are strapped with unnecessary debt, take a class now on budgeting and managing money. I recommend the Financial Peace program by Dave Ramsey, but there are many good and inexpensive options. In fact, in my chapter on Networking, I discuss many FREE options for getting out and meeting contacts who can lead you to job opportunities. Throughout this workbook, I will lean toward free or inexpensive methods. In the meantime, secure your finances and prepare for a tight ride.

Take Control of your Finances During your Job Search, or your Finances will Control your Job Search

As I listened to Dave Ramsey say, "You have to make money behave," in one of his Financial Peace Workshops, I thought, "Do I control my expenses, or do they control me?" Now as I think through the planning involved in Career Transition, it becomes clear that you can take control of your finances during your job search, or your finances will control your job search.

You have a number of choices to make:
- ✓ in which job search resources you will invest,
- ✓ which networking events you might attend,
- ✓ what opportunities you will pursue, and ultimately,
- ✓ how you will negotiate for a fair offer from your next employer.

If you have your finances secure, you will be able to make the choices you want to make, instead of those you are forced to make. Here are 3 tips to start you on the right path:

1. Plan to Reduce Your Expenses.

You might consider this a burden, or you might consider it an opportunity. Think about how you can reduce your monthly budget and start cutting those costs NOW, before they mount into your growing debt. On the next page you will find a budget-cutting worksheet. PLEASE DON'T SKIP THIS!

2. Continue the Discipline of Saving.

Dave Ramsey would also start you out on a simple path. His "Baby Steps" start with saving, which is a discipline that begins a harvest of peace. You might not consider a time of career transition, especially if you are in between jobs, a time to begin saving. Consider at least "Baby Step 1", to set aside and maintain a minimum of $1000 in savings.

3. Create a Detailed Budget.

If you have not worked out a detailed budget, it's critical you do so during career transition. Every dollar should have a name on it before the month begins. Chart out your fixed expenses, your variable expenses, and your "God Only Knows" (unexpected emergency) expenses.

Don't let all this work go to waste by "pity party" spending, lonely spending, or unexpected emergencies. There are no unexpected emergencies when you have planned for them. Start practicing that beautiful ancient word, "No," and remember that "it's not in the budget" is also a perfectly acceptable response.

 *The STAR Career Workbook*

BUDGET CUTTING WORKSHEET

Think through how you can reduce your monthly budget and start cutting those costs NOW, before they mount into growing debt.

Expense Item	Current Expense ($)	Amount to Reduce ($)
Cable or Satellite TV (cut the cord!)		
Internet Access – **it is a must**, but can you reduce? Find Free Wi-Fi, but not with $5 coffee!		
Home Phone (do you really use this anymore?)		
Cell Phone (reduce data use)		
Utilities (reduce power consumption)		
Groceries (shop wisely, use coupons)		
Gasoline (reduce unnecessary travel and use public transportation when possible)		
Recreational / Fitness (put gym membership on hold and work out at home)		
Clothing / Dry Cleaning / Personal Care (shop less and do more of it yourself)		
Charity (unfortunately, you may need to partially cut back, but tithing may still be possible)		
Memberships, Subscriptions, Dues		
Gifts (get crafty or get simple)		
Other:		
Total Possible Monthly Savings:	⟶	

 *The STAR Career Workbook*

Assessing Your Values, Strengths, Virtues, and Vision

Identifying, Clarifying, Comparing, and Learning from your Values
Your core values identify your areas of passion. These are the fundamentals of what you believe. They are partially derived from faith and heritage, and partially from your life experiences.

Your core values must be consistent with an organization you join, if you wish to stay there for long, and if you wish to advance into more senior roles in that organization.

In later sections, I will talk about how you go about the process of identifying an organization's core values, but first you must identify, clarify, and learn from your own. The exercises in this chapter will have you identify, test and compare your values.

Identifying and Owning your Core Strengths
I firmly believe that you should "stick with what you know". I tell my career search clients to leverage their current education, training, and experience. I do not advocate making a drastic career change, unless your field is simply dying, or staying in it would require relocation or other changes you cannot make. If you have to make some type of change, stay in a relevant field and leverage your key accomplishments and strengths.

In the exercises in this chapter, you will identify your key strengths, most of which you have been developing since childhood. Not only are you challenged with identifying them, but you are challenged with understanding how you have maximized them for career development

 **The STAR Career Workbook**

and career advancement. In the chapter on the STAR Communication Strategy, you will learn how to communicate those core strengths to contacts, references, lead sources, recruiters, and hiring managers.

Identifying your Signature Virtues and Applying Those to your Career
As I will later discuss, while a company is evaluating you, you should also be evaluating them. I will teach you how to use 4 key metrics, compatibility, chemistry, character, and compensation. Your signature virtues are the areas that define your character. You can compare those virtues to the espoused and activated corporate character at your target employers. The simple exercise I have for you in this chapter is just a start. You might consider further reading on character, principles and traits, and possibly a personality assessment such as the Myers-Briggs Type Indicator or the DISC Personality Profile.

Identifying your Career Vision
To cut your teeth on defining and directing your career search, I begin with a look at the end. Casting your Career Vision is an exercise to clarify your direction, motivate yourself toward that goal, and build passion in your future communication with others.

Instructions: Identifying Core Values Worksheet

1. From the list of values on the next page, place 1 star next to the 10 values that are most important to you. Add any values of your own to the list at the bottom of the worksheet and place a star next to these as well.
2. After you have identified your top 10, place a 2nd star next to your top 5 values.
3. Finally, identify your top 3 values by placing a 3rd star next to your top 3. These would be your central core values, the values you would bring forward into a Mission or Vision Statement.

 *The STAR Career Workbook*

Identifying Core Values Worksheet

Achievement	Fame	Power
Advancement	Family	Privacy
Adventure	Growth	Purity
Affection	Harmony	Quality
Accountability	Integrity	Relationships
Challenges	Independence	Responsibility
Change	Influence	Recognition
Community	Intellect	Religion
Competence	Involvement	Reputation
Competition	Leadership	Security
Cooperation	Location	Service
Creativity	Loyalty	Self-respect
Decision-making	Meaningful work	Sophistication
Democracy	Merit	Stability
Economic security	Nature	Time
Efficiency	Order	Wealth
Ethical practice	Peace	Work Ethic
Excellence	Physical Challenge	Teamwork
Excitement	Pleasure	Wisdom

Adapted from: C. Roberts, Fifth Discipline Field book

Values Testing

PURPOSE: This values test helps you understand the strength of each of your stated core values. This activity also indicates what steps you should take in order to develop stronger and clearer values.

INSTRUCTIONS: From the previous exercise enter your top 10 values, with your top 3 in the number 1 through 3 slots, and the rest from 4 through 10 in no particular order. If you do not have time to address top 10 values now, make sure you at least cover your top 3 and come back to the rest later.

	Value	1	2	3	4	5	6	7
1								
2								
3								
4								
5								
6								
7								
8								
9								
10								

The 7 numbers heading the columns on the right-hand side of the grid represent the following 7 questions:
1. Are you proud of (do you prize or cherish) this value?
2. Have you publicly affirmed this value?
3. Have you chosen this value from *alternatives*?

The STAR Career Workbook

4. Have you chosen this value after *thoughtful consideration* of the pros and cons, and consequences?
5. Have you chosen this value *freely*?
6. Have you *acted* or done anything about your beliefs?
7. Have you acted with *repetition*, pattern, or consistency on this value?

Answer each of these 7 questions in relation to each value. If you have a positive response to the questions on top, put a star in each appropriate box. If you cannot answer each question affirmatively, leave the box blank.

Just the simple visualization of how many stars you have next to your listed values will give you an idea of how truly important this value is to you. You may still strongly believe in a value for which you have fewer stars, indicating that this is an area where you need to challenge yourself going forward.

Adapted from: Values Clarification by Dr. Sidney B. Simon, Dr. Leland W. Howe, and Dr. Howard Kirschehbaum, Warner Books, NY, 1995

# The STAR Career Workbook

In Search of Excellence

In Thomas J. Peters and Robert H. Waterman Jr.'s 1982 best-selling book, In Search of Excellence, they found that the best-run American companies use 8 core values to stay on top. How do your personal values compare?

1. A bias for action: preference for doing something/anything, rather than sending a question through cycles and cycles of analyses and committee reports.
2. Staying close to the customer: learning his preference and catering to them. Seeking a win-win solution rather than pushing the customer to take my solutions.
3. Autonomy and entrepreneurship: breaking the corporation (or my team, my job, my plans) into small companies (parts), and encouraging them to think independently and competitively.
4. Productivity through people: creating in all employees the awareness that their best efforts are essential, and that they will share in the rewards of the company's success.
5. Hands-on, value driven: insisting that executives (I) keep in touch with the firm's essential values, beliefs, systems, and business.
6. Stick to the best knitting: remaining with the business (core strengths) the company (I) know(s) best.
7. Simple form, lean staff: few administrative layers, few people at upper levels. (Keep it simple – don't try to be a "jack of all trades.")
8. Simultaneous loose/tight properties: fostering a climate where there is a dedication to central values, combined with tolerance for all employees who accept those values. (Comfortable with ambiguity, uncertainty, and change).

# The STAR Career Workbook

Find Out What You Do Well and Do More of It

STRENGTHS: A DEFINITION

Basically, strengths are the things you do well. On a more sophisticated level, a strength is a pattern of behavior, thoughts, and feelings that produces a high degree of satisfaction and pride; generates both physical and/or financial reward; and presents measurable progress toward excellence.

STRENGTHS IDENTIFICATION WORKSHEET

Instructions:

Step 1: Write your strengths in the <u>middle</u> column, below each characteristic. You may repeat some strengths under different characteristics; this clarifies it as a strength. You will use the small columns on the left and right, after documenting your strengths.

Step 2: Go back and put a star in the left-hand column next to any strength for which you've received an award, letter of recognition, or write-up in a newsletter or some type of publication.

Step 3: Go back and put a star (or another star) in the left-hand column next to any strength through which you helped to improve the "bottom-line" of your past employer, through cost savings, profits, time reduction, etc.

Step 4: Go back and rank (in the right-hand column) your strengths, from 1 being the one that you believe describes you the best, to the last.

The STAR Career Workbook

THE FIVE CHARACTERISTICS OF A STRENGTH

ONE: LISTEN FOR YEARNINGS

Characterized as the pull or attraction to one activity over another, a process that begins in early childhood. Think of a yearning you have in your work, the things you look forward to working on, or that draw you back.

TWO: WATCH FOR SATISFACTIONS

Satisfactions are those experiences where the emotional and physical rewards are great. Competencies and satisfactions are not always partners. If it doesn't feel good you are not practicing a strength. Think of the things you do at work that consistently bring satisfaction.

The STAR Career Workbook

THREE: WATCH FOR RAPID LEARNING

If you catch on quickly to something, you're likely to be good at it. Naturals are those who learn by "jumping in". Slow learning, however, is evidence of a non-strength. Think of things you pick up very quickly at work. Within days, or even hours, others are asking you to show them how to do it.

FOUR: GLIMPSES OF EXCELLENCE

You can spot a strength by glimpsing a moment of excellence within a performance. Only the trained eye can glimpse moments of excellence. One of the most effective ways to master this technique is by studying success. Think of things you've done when you were complimented on your excellence, when someone used words like, "perfect, excellent job, or well-done".

The STAR Career Workbook

FIVE: TOTAL PERFORMANCE OF EXCELLENCE

Total performance of excellence is a flow of successful behavior, when there are no conscious steps in the mind of the performer. Total performance isn't a glimpse, but the complete extension of an activity. It doesn't happen occasionally, but, rather, each time the activity is performed.

One final test of total performance is the improvement of activity over a period of time. The satisfaction gained by total performance will cause a person to want to repeat it, but with repetition must come improvement. Think of times when you have "lost yourself" in the execution of your work, when the effort was effortless, and the success was repeatable and sustainable.

Later in this book, you will be asked to identify your STAR stories of success for your marketing materials and resume. The items you are documenting here will prepare you to populate those worksheets.

Adapted from: Soar With Your Strengths, Donald O. Clifton and Paula Nelson, Bantam Doubleday Dell, NY, 1992

The STAR Career Workbook

Signature Virtues, Self-Rating Scale

✹ Please read the descriptions of the virtues (or character traits) on the following pages. As you read them, write a plus sign (+) in the margin next to the ones that you think describe you well. Write a minus sign (-) in the margin next to the ones that you think do <u>not</u> describe you well. Leave the rest unmarked.

✹ Then look through the ones with a plus sign (+) next to them, and try to rank order your top 5. That is, place a "1" in the left-hand column for the one that you think BEST describes you, then a "2" in the next best one, etc.

✹ Finally, look through the ones with a minus sign (-) in the margin and try to rank the 5 that are LEAST true or applicable to you. Put a "24" next to the one that is least like you, then a "23", etc.

✹ **Later in this workbook, you will be asked to work on your Professional Introduction, and you will draft elevator pitches and cover letters which introduce you to target networking contacts. Your work here will prepare you to populate those worksheets.**

The STAR Career Workbook

+ or -	Virtue	Description
	Curiosity Rank_____	You are curious about the world and you strongly desire the experience of it. You are flexible about matters that don't fit your preconceptions. Curious people do not simply tolerate ambiguity, but they like it and are intrigued by it. You seek out novelty, and you are rarely bored.
	Learning Rank_____	You love learning new things, whether you are in a class or on your own. There are domains of knowledge in which you are the expert, and others value your expertise. You love learning about these domains, even in the absence of any external incentives to do so.
	Judgment Rank_____	You think things through and examine them from all sides. You do not jump to conclusions, and you rely only on solid evidence to make your decisions. You are able to change your mind. You are very good at sifting information objectively and rationally.
	Ingenuity Rank_____	When you are faced with something you want, you are outstanding at finding novel, yet appropriate behavior, to reach that goal. You are rarely content with doing something the conventional way. This strength is also called "practical intelligence" or more bluntly common sense or street smarts.

 **The STAR Career Workbook**

+ or -	Virtue	Description
	Emotional Intelligence Rank_____	You are aware of the motives and feelings of others, and of yourself, and you can respond skillfully. You notice differences among others, especially with respect to their moods, temperaments, motivations, and intentions, and then you <u>act</u> upon these distinctions. You also have finely-tuned access to your own feelings, and the ability to use that knowledge to understand and guide your behavior.
	Perspective Rank_____	You have a way of looking at the world that makes sense to others and yourself. Others seek you out to draw on your experience, and you are often able to help them solve problems and gain perspective. You have a good sense of what is really important in life.
	Valor Rank_____	You do not shrink from threat, challenge, pain, or difficulty. Valor is more than bravery during physical threat. It refers, as well, to intellectual or emotional stances that are unpopular, difficult, or dangerous. The brave person is able to uncouple the emotional and behavioral components of fear, resisting the urge to flee, and facing the fearful situation.

The STAR Career Workbook

+ or -	Virtue	Description
	Perseverance Rank_____	You finish what you start. You take on difficult projects and finish them, usually with good cheer and minimal complaint. You do what you say you will do, and sometimes more, never less. Perseverance does not mean dogged or obsessive pursuit of unattainable goals. Rather, you remain flexible, realistic, and not perfectionistic.
	Integrity Rank_____	You are an honest person, not only always speaking the truth, but also living your life in a genuine and authentic way. You are down-to-earth and without pretense. You represent your intentions and commitments to others, and to yourself, in sincere fashion, whether by word or deed.
	Kindness Rank_____	You are kind and generous to others, and you are never too busy to do a favor. You enjoy doing good deeds for others, even if you do not know them well. Your actions are very often guided by other people's best interests, even when these override your own immediate wishes and needs.
	Loving Rank_____	You value close and intimate relationships with others. You have deep and sustained feelings for others, who feel the same way about you. This strength is more than the Western notion of romance; it is about very deep ties to several or many people.

The STAR Career Workbook

+ or -	Virtue	Description
	Teamwork Rank_____	You excel as a member of a group. You are a loyal and dedicated teammate. You always do your share, and you work hard for the success of the group. You value the group goals and purposes even when they differ from your own. You respect those who are rightfully in positions of authority.
	Fairness Rank_____	You do not let your personal feelings bias your decisions about other people. You give everyone a chance. You take the welfare of others, even those you do not know personally, as seriously as your own, and you can easily set aside personal prejudices.
	Leadership Rank_____	You do a good job organizing activities and seeing to it that they happen. You are a humane and effective leader, attending to getting the group's work, at the same time as, maintaining good relations among group members. You are additionally humane when you handle intergroup relations "with malice toward none and charity toward all."
	Self-control Rank_____	You can easily hold your desires, needs, and impulses in check when it is appropriate. It is not enough to know what is correct; you must also be able to put this knowledge into action. When something bad happens, you can regulate your own emotions. You can repair and neutralize your negative feelings, and generate positive emotions on your own.

The STAR Career Workbook

+ or -	Virtue	Description
	Prudence Rank_____	You are a careful person. You do not say or do things you might later regret. You wait until all the votes are in before embarking on a course of action. You are far-sighted and deliberative. You are good at resisting impulses about short term goals, for the sake of longer term success.
	Humility Rank_____	You do not seek the spotlight, preferring to let your accomplishments speak for themselves. You do not regard yourself as special, and others recognize and value your modesty. You are unpretentious. You see your own aspirations, victories, and defeats, as pretty unimportant in the larger scheme of things.
	Appreciation Rank_____	You stop and smell the roses. You appreciate beauty, excellence, and skill in all domains: nature, the arts, science, and the wide range of abilities that other people possess. You often see or hear things that cause you to feel profound feelings of awe and wonder.
	Gratitude Rank_____	You are aware of the good things that happen to you, and you never take them for granted. You always take the time to express your thanks. Gratitude is an appreciation of someone else's excellence in moral character. Gratitude can also be directed toward impersonal and nonhuman sources--God, nature, life, etc.

The STAR Career Workbook

+ or -	Virtue	Description
	Hope Rank_____	You expect the best in the future, and you plan and work in order to achieve it. Hope, optimism, and future-mindedness are yours. Expecting that good events will occur, you sustain good cheer in the here-and-now, and galvanize a goal-directed life.
	Spirituality Rank_____	You have strong and coherent beliefs about the higher purpose and meaning of all things. You know where you fit in the larger scheme. Your beliefs shape your actions, and are a source of comfort to you.
	Grace Rank_____	You forgive those who have done you wrong. You always give people a second chance. Your guiding principle is mercy and not revenge. When offended or hurt by someone else, through forgiveness, your motivations and actions regarding the transgressor, become benevolent, kind, and generous.
	Humor Rank_____	You like to laugh and bring smiles to other people. You can easily see the light side of life. You are playful and funny.
	Zeal Rank_____	You are a spirited person. You throw yourself body and soul into the activities you undertake. You wake up in the morning looking forward to the day. The passion that you bring to activities is infectious.

(Adapted from Jonathan Haidt's work of Martin E.P. Seligman's 2002: <u>Authentic Happiness</u>)

# The STAR Career Workbook

I Learned Statements

As a follow-up to the values clarification done previously, complete the sentences below. Add additional thoughts you find helpful. Then take a few minutes to reflect on what you have learned or discovered, and how it might affect your career search. Keep this list handy so that you can come back and make notes, as you recall future learning. **Don't skip this!!** Many readers do, and as a result, miss a valuable exercise. Statements should be kept short and to the point. Focus on personal learning rather than on general, intellectualized learning.

- I learned that I...

- I relearned that I...

- I was surprised that I...

- I was pleased that I...

- I was displeased that I...

- I am more motivated than ever to...

- I want to work more on my...

- I have discussed/will discuss with _____ my thoughts about ...

Adapted from: Values Clarification, by Dr. Sidney B. Simon, Dr. Leland W. Howe, and Dr. Howard Kirschenbaum, Warner Books, NY, 1995

 **The STAR Career Workbook**

Casting your Career Vision

Stephen Covey, author of the bestseller "The 7 Habits of Highly Effective People", says, "Begin with the end in mind." What is the end-result you are looking for? You may respond with "Duh, I need a job." If that is all you are asking for, then that is all you will get. The Bible reminds me that if I have faith and do not doubt *what God wants to do* through me, I can say to the mountain, "be lifted up and thrown into the sea," and it will happen! (Matthew 21:21)

Your end-result needs to be a better vision, an inspiring goal – you are the new CEO of your job search, of your career. What is *your* vision for *your* future? Great leaders cast a vision that their followers can identify and pursue. They use language that is **inspiring** and **powerful.**

In later steps, you will integrate your vision and mission into your Professional Objective and Professional Introduction. So, thinking through the inspiring way you want to frame your future now, will make those communication strategies even more powerful.

Name Your Target: Identify the title or titles you wish to pursue. But don't just sit on a title you are familiar with; strive for a higher calling. Include language that is inspiring. **Example:** "HR Generalist" becomes "Senior Human Resources Business Partner". And "Product Manager" becomes "Senior Product Evangelist".

What is your aspirational title? Draft 2 or 3 if you are inspired to do so.

The STAR Career Workbook

Your Role in That Vision: Cast a vision for the role you will play, and build in responsibilities, that are above and beyond what you've done up to now.

Examples: As a project manager with experience delivering key software releases, you might cast a vision of "responsible for global delivery of critical software solutions, that change the way the world uses the internet."

What is your aspirational role? What is the BIG thing you are going to do with your next career?

[ ]

INTEGRATING YOUR VALUES, STRENGTHS, AND VIRTUES: With all the work you've done on Values Clarification and Strengths Identification, what are the values and strengths you wish to instill into your career path going forward? On the next page, you will bring all of this together.

The STAR Career Workbook

Casting your Career Vision (continued)

Take some time now to write your Career Vision here. You will bring it forward later, into your *Professional Objective, Professional Introduction, and Marketing Plan*

I am pursuing my vision of becoming a…	
In a role where I am responsible for…	
In this role I will be able to demonstrate my virtues, including…	
And my strengths including…	
With an organization consistent with my core values of…	

The STAR Career Workbook

The STAR Communication Strategy

The communication strategy that follows is developed to help both the traditional job application process **and** networking toward hidden employment opportunities. However, my preference for you is that you **network** for your next career move.

"Staying on Message"

I believe the most important element to your communication strategy is "staying on message". It is the same as branding, from a marketing perspective, or messaging from a public relations perspective. The tools you will develop to help you stay on message include:

1. Moving Forward Statement
2. Professional Introduction
3. Professional Objective
4. STAR stories (statements of key accomplishments) – 3 for each job on your resume

Your Communications Package

In the following pages I will guide you in the drafting and improvement of:

- A. Resume (s)
- B. Cover Letters
- C. Introduction Letters
- D. Recommendation Letters
- E. References
- F. Job Applications

The STAR Career Workbook

Moving Forward Statement

Your Moving Forward Statement (sometimes referred to as an "Exit Statement") is a brief statement about why you are making a career transition.

It may include some brief information about your previous position and employer, and especially your role there (so long as it corresponds with your career pursuit), but it should include "moving forward" language to indicate where you are heading.

Remember to pull in your Career Vision work, your core values and your strengths.

You will use this statement in:
- Networking Meetings: letting them know your target roles in their companies, or places where they can refer you.
- Casual Conversations: at happy hours, professional meetings, and family gatherings, as you are discussing your plans, and getting buy-in from your support network.
- Often, this is the first question a recruiter will ask you on the phone ("Why are you looking?").

The STAR Career Workbook

Draft your MOVING FORWARD STATEMENT here:

After a rewarding _____ years in the _____

industry, and recent positions (titles) of _____ and

_____, I am moving forward to a role as

_____ (use your "visionary" title you're

your earlier work) within a _____ (name the

industry, size and/or key attribute, like "fast-growing" or "B2B")

organization, where I can offer my expertise in

_____ and _____

(name your top 2 STRENGTHS from your earlier work). I am leaving (or

looking to leave) my current employer due to

_____ (keep it simple, like

"a reduction in force due to a recent merger.")

Or use the following space to map out your own..........

 ## The STAR Career Workbook

Moving Forward Statement Samples:

- After a recent opportunity to work with a leading online security tech company, and due to a recent restructuring, I am moving forward to pursue a Senior Marketing Management position in a B2B online business.

- Due to the economic conditions nationwide, my former employer was forced to let a number of us go, so I am moving forward in my career progression, toward a role as a Senior Software Engineer, where I can continue to deliver outstanding products in record time.

- After a fulfilling 20 years within the semiconductor industry, and recent positions in management and product ownership, I am moving on to a leadership role within a small engineering or product development organization, where I can offer my expertise in product-to-customer alignment and cost-saving engineering practices.

Professional Introduction

Your Professional Introduction is your key tool in your communication strategy. It is often referred to as a positioning statement or an elevator speech. Picture yourself stepping onto an elevator, alone, with the CEO of one of your target employers. What will you say? You will use this statement in your:

- Resume: incorporated into your Professional Summary / Overview
- Networking Meetings: letting them know your target roles in their companies, or places where they can refer you.
- Casual Conversations: at happy hours, professional meetings, and family gatherings, as you are discussing your plans and getting buy-in from your support network.
- Interviewing: rehearsed, so that you stay on message and are clear about your objectives.

I am a (profession/title)	
With expertise in	
and	
My education includes	
I have worked in industries including	
and	
and I have had success at	
(1 -3 bottom-line results items)	

See examples on the following Page

The STAR Career Workbook

Professional Introduction Examples:

- I am a Senior Marketing Manager with expertise in online businesses, including B2B and B2C, and industries including online security, travel, e-commerce, media, and higher education. My passion is creating information and technology that enlightens people's lives. I have been successful at pulling together human, financial, and physical resources, to achieve business goals. I am a mediator and facilitator who moves projects forward with integrity and discipline.

- I am a Senior Human Resources Business Partner with expert consulting skills on HR strategy and People ROI. I am skilled in financial analysis, have strong business acumen, and I have full lifecycle project management experience. I have worked in industries including Information Technology, State and Federal Government, and Recruiting and Staffing. I have had success at reducing cost through lean practices in recruiting, benefits, and HR administration; and I have increased retention of desired talent through smarter performance reviews and professional development programs.

Or use the following space to map out your own……….

Professional Objective

Your Professional Objective is an internal tool that you will use in identifying your goals, and in communicating those goals with your network. It is not recommended for your resume. Instead, you will use your Professional Introduction at the top of your resume (more on that later). You will use this statement in:

- Networking Calls: help your contact understand how they can direct you.
- Casual Conversations: at happy hours, association meetings, and family gatherings, as you are discussing your plans, and getting buy-in from your support network.
- Recruiter Phone Screens and Interviewing: rehearsed, so that you stay on message, and are clear about your objectives.

I am seeking a role as a (profession/title)	
in industries such as	
or	
where I can exercise my expertise in	
and	
and repeat my success at	
(1-3 bottom-line results items)	

 **The STAR Career Workbook**

Examples on the next page
Professional Objective Examples:

- I am looking for a Senior Marketing Management position in online business, B2B or B2C, where I can help create information and technology that enlightens people's lives. I would like to be in a role that allows me to facilitate work integration, and lead teams with integrity and discipline.

- I am seeking an opportunity to create profit for a fast-growing semiconductor or electronics manufacturing company, where I can leverage my 15 years of quota-busting sales experience in the commercial and consumer space. I have developed over $6M in revenue streams with major OEMs, like HP and Dell, and sell-through strategies to major retailers, like Best-Buy and Staples.

Or use the following space to map out your own……….

The STAR Career Workbook

Identifying your Key Accomplishments

It is important in your communication strategy to have clearly identified key accomplishment statements. You will use these statements in:
- Resume: condensed bullets
- Networking Calls: gaining interest by recalling a specific accomplishment relevant to your target
- Casual Conversations: at happy hours, association meetings, and family gatherings, as you are discussing your plans, and getting buy-in from your support network.
- Interviewing: rehearsed answers that keep you "on message" with your target position.

The STAR Method of Accomplishment Stories

(Statements of key accomplishments)
3 for each job on your resume

Just as a great novel or movie has a crisis, a great success story has a challenge. Characters with depth, and stories with heart, involve trials and challenges. Business leaders got where they are by using their resources to overcome these trials. They want to know how you've overcome adversity. In a STAR story, you will explain the pain of the difficulty or barrier you faced, and then how you climbed over that mountain.

I have researched the various methods developed by leading outplacement specialists and recruiting experts, and developed the following, easy-to-remember method...

The STAR Career Workbook

Situation: describe the job you were in and your responsibility

Trial: describe a barrier or difficulty you faced

Actions: describe the action you took to address the trial.

Results: describe the results you achieved which helped the company's bottom line using *Hard Numbers*: i.e. dollars, percentages, time, headcount, etc.

Relevance:

STAR stories are used when they most directly connect to the business, needs, issues, or industry of the listener or target. **In a happy hour**, you would discuss STAR stories that relate to the companies you want people to introduce you to. **In a networking call**, you would relate a story that grabs attention of the person you are calling, which would be relevant to his/her industry and business needs. **In an interview**, you would use a STAR story that is relevant to the industry and business needs of your host, and which ***most closely*** answers the question of the interviewer.

STAR Worksheets

In the STAR Worksheets on the following pages, take some time now to document your key accomplishments, using this methodology.

Try to document 4 accomplishments for your most recent position, and 2 more accomplishments for your following 2 positions.

The STAR Career Workbook

STAR Story Example:

I was promoted to HR Director for a small technology firm, and my first challenge was to renew our corporate benefits plans. Our renewal date was August 1. It was May and nothing had been done. I had no notes, except a list of benefits brokers to call. But most painfully, I had a renewal offer from our current broker, with a 26% increase in rates! For our small company, this was about $400,000 in added cost. I analyzed our current plan utilization across the country, and assessed new products and services we could integrate into our plan, to save cost and create efficiencies. I negotiated with multiple vendors, and communicated my plans and progress throughout the organization, to reduce stress about the pending changes. I secured a new plan utilizing a nationwide PPO plan, with advantageous rates for lower risk areas and employees who chose health-improvement plans. I worked in an HSA to offset a new higher deductible option, in which many of our younger engineers had expressed interest, and achieved a 10% savings against our previous year. This represented an overall savings of 36% (around ½ million dollars) to the company.

Resume Bullet:

- After promotion to HR Director, inherited an overdue benefits renewal project and a 26% increase in rates. Analyzed plan, selected creative new solutions, renegotiated with vendors, and communicated changes throughout company. Achieved an overall savings of 36%.

Shorter, Power-Packed Resume Bullet:

- Achieved an overall savings of 36% on benefits renewal using creative new solutions. Rigorous negotiation with vendors and consistent communication throughout company.

 *The STAR Career Workbook*

STAR Worksheets

Job	
Situation	
Trial	
Action	
Results	
Bullet (use later)	

Job	
Situation	
Trial	
Action	
Results	
Bullet (use later)	

The STAR Career Workbook

STAR Worksheets

Job	
Situation	
Trial	
Action	
Results	
Bullet (use later)	

Job	
Situation	
Trial	
Action	
Results	
Bullet (use later)	

The STAR Career Workbook

STAR Worksheets

Job	
Situation	
Trial	
Action	
Results	
Bullet (use later)	

Job	
Situation	
Trial	
Action	
Results	
Bullet (use later)	

# The STAR Career Workbook

STAR Worksheets

Job	
Situation	
Trial	
Action	
Results	
Bullet (use later)	

Job	
Situation	
Trial	
Action	
Results	
Bullet (use later)	

The STAR Career Workbook

Developing a STAR Resume

Your Resume – What is it good for?

There are things you should expect your resume to do for you and things you should not expect it to do. Having a realistic understanding of the function and capability of this tool is important in driving your efforts toward success. First, your resume will not get you a job. Your resume **might** get you a phone call, but it alone will not even get you an interview. Your resume is simply one tool in your communications package that communicates your "message". You have to deliver that message persistently and consistently.

Your resume is a sales brochure: Your resume sells "product you". Companies, industries, and markets have critical needs, and your resume should communicate your **value** and **benefits** as a solution to those needs. Those benefits are found in the clear identification of your expertise and passion. That value is found in the identifiable, bottom-line results of your key successes.

Your resume is a conversation opener: Your resume answers the question, "why should I call you?" But it is just a conversation opener, not the entire conversation. Your resume cannot, and should not, cover every detail of your working life. It needs to be **brief**, succinct, and **relevant** to the path(s) you are pursuing. And it should leave just enough room for questions in that continuing conversation.

Your resume is a foot in the door: Like the executive's favorite coffee mug he received from his favorite sales rep, your resume is a "leave-behind" that reminds the employer of your compatibility, chemistry, and connection with their organization. For this reason, it must be **attractive, functional,** and **complete.**

Your resume is a first impression: Your resume is often your first chance to get in front of a hiring manager (virtually speaking). If you have followed my guidance and networked sufficiently within the organization, your name, credentials, and compatibility will have already been floated by this hiring manager. Whether you have done this or not, all bets are off when he pulls open your resume on his computer screen.

As first impressions go, make it count – because you only get one.

It is tempting therefore to try and include everything you can think of that any employer would want to know about you. But consider the time, attention, pains, and needs of the hiring manager. Your resume therefore should be **targeted** to your market and **consistent** with your message – nothing more.

Your resume is an interview guide: A well-written resume will be used by the employer throughout your forthcoming interviews. They will generate their questions based on what they read in this document. *Have you mentioned anything you don't want to talk about?*

Your resume should be **success/solution-focused**, and **directive** to the reader toward topics you are prepared to talk about.

Using bullet points that highlight your areas of expertise, your strengths and passions, and your **key successes**, your interview will be filled with energy as you are asked to expand on topics which you remember well, and about which you enjoy speaking.

The STAR Career Workbook

Best Practices for an Impactful Resume

Header and Contact Information

Your contact information on your resume should be accurate. You may choose not to list a full address, but to only indicate your city and state of residence. You may even use the name of the metropolitan area where you live.

However, make sure you indicate your location in some way. Recruiters, in particular need to know this information. If they have to guess or hunt for your location, they might give up and reject your application. Today, with cell phone numbers carrying forward with us year over year, recruiters may assume you are in the metropolitan area that matches the area code for your mobile number. If this is not the case, you are in for some confusion. Please tell them where you are!

Use a professional-sounding email address (not a nickname, and nothing potentially distasteful to anyone). I prefer that you have your whole name in the address (i.e. dan.medlin@xmail.com). This has become more critical with the use of Applicant Tracking Systems and template emails. Your email address may be the only way the recruiter or hiring manager can differentiate you during their screening or communications.

Use only one email address and one phone number. Use the phone number you will check most often, and where you have the best voicemail system. A mobile phone is often the best choice as you can also capture the phone number of the person who called you, and save numbers into your contacts quickly and easily for follow-up.

Full CVs in Europe and Asia often include a photo and some personal data, such as marital status, date of birth, and more. Clearly, you would not provide this material inside the United States. But if you are outside

of the United States, or applying to a role overseas, default to the norms of that country.

Professional Summary or Introduction

I do not recommend posting your professional objective at the top of your resume, but instead, launching into your Professional Summary (or Professional Introduction). The professional summary answers the question for the reader, "should I continue reading this resume?" Your goal is to capture the attention of the reader with an impactful overview of how you match their needs.

Resume Body and Content

The body of your resume should be typed in First Person (without personal pronouns), and in Past Tense. Keep it consistent. See the samples and worksheets in the following pages for how this looks.

Note that some experts today are advocating more personalized, testimonial content. I support this in your Professional Summary or Introduction, but not throughout the resume as it will add too much content and softens the impact.

Your resume should be stripped of personal pronouns ("I," "my," "we," "they," etc.) so that sentences begin with action words, or power verbs. See the chart of power verbs later. Make sure to alternate the use of similar action words – or **power verbs,** so that your resume is not repetitive and boring.

If you are not sure of the exact meaning of a word, look it up!

Use the language and acronyms that are specific to your industry *(see Exception for Military Transitions),* but not to the level that an outsider cannot understand what you've done, where you've been, and what you've accomplished. Some explaining may be needed for very esoteric terms. Don't hesitate to spell out an acronym and provide alternate versions of the same term, which are popular in your industry.

The STAR Career Workbook

Content Exception for Military Transitions: Your service to our country is incredibly appreciated, but the technical and functional terminology in your resume needs to be translated into civilian language. Spend some time with your base transition counselor to help, and ask if there are industry partners willing to review your resume again. A phone call or meeting with an industry partner may also help you with leads to great job opportunities!

Editing and Corrections

Complete sentences are not critical but accurate grammar and spelling ARE. Use your word processing software to check your spelling and grammar. Note that your software will tell you that you have many incomplete sentences because you have stripped out the nouns and pronouns. This is OK. Make sure you review all recommendations by the software and correct every misspelling. Look for very obvious things, like the spelling of your home city. Remember that your own eyes can trick you!

Ensure that you have no red or green lines embedded in your document from MS Word's spell-check and grammar check, before you send your resume. If you send your resume as a Word document, these same lines will appear on the other side! You can clear these lines by choosing "ignore" during spell and grammar check, for any technical terms, acronyms, or incomplete sentences you wish to leave in place.

Do not rely completely on your word processor's spell check! Ask a friend or two to review your resume for additional errors, and in the meantime, ask them to give a strong critique of your choice of words, positioning of statements, etc. The more "smart eyes" you can have look over your resume the better.

Color and Artwork

Do not use colors, fancy designs, artwork, or pictures (of yourself or anyone else) on your resume. Exceptions would be made for graphic artists, traditional artists, photographers, and other creative professionals. However, even these professionals should lean toward presenting the more creative material in an online setting via a web portfolio, and keep the resume clean and crisp for capturing key information.

Job History

It is not necessary to list every job you have held, but **gaps in employment** should be notated with a reasonable explanation.

Example: Took 2 years off to work a mission overseas.

Integrate that experience into your chronological professional history, with a brief overview of your role and any key accomplishments.

All jobs belonging to one employer (showing career progression and adaptability within an organization), should appear under a master heading for that employer (showing longevity with that employer, which is becoming rare). The master heading would have the full time frame (year to year) you were at that employer. Each separate role with this employer would appear underneath the master heading and would specify the years you were in that role.

Leave months started and ended off of job dates. It rounds out your years of service, eliminates potential red flags for gatekeepers, and leaves room for discussion in interviews.

Leave years of education off of resume. This prevents age bias on either end, whether you are young or old, and if you started and stopped, or returned for a degree, it eliminates red flag issues for gatekeepers. In a screening or interview you will have an opportunity to specify the dates of your education. Once you've moved through the resume screening gate to an interview, you can overcome possible objections or bias by addressing your accomplishments and strengths.

 *The STAR Career Workbook*

Use STAR Bullets!

The bullet points under each job listing should be focused on work-based contributions, or accomplishments, and less on general job duties. These accomplishment bullets should include both the action you took, and the results for the organization, and should clearly identify your role in the effort. Refer back to the work you did with your STAR stories in the section on The STAR Method of Accomplishment Stories. You will learn more in a few pages, how you can "bulletize" these stories and place them in your resume, under your job history. This work will be done in the section called "Driving Attention to Your Success Using STAR Bullets.

Resume Ending

Do not bother with saying "References Available on Request" at the bottom of your resume. It is a waste of space. They will ask for references if they want to pursue you and you will want to provide them if they ask.

Last Recommendation

I also recommend that you convert your resume to PDF. This secures the formatting, and prevents someone from making changes to the source document. You will use this version mostly when you are networking and sending your resume to internal contacts, people who might refer or recommend you, or directly to hiring managers, when you can reach them. Most recruiters can copy information they may need from a PDF document, like a phone number or email address.

Most resume parsing software in advanced Applicant Tracking Systems (ATS) can now convert data from PDF. **However**, be prepared to review and edit the data after it is uploaded. If you are spending too much time

editing data in an ATS, after uploading a PDF, you may want to upload your resume as an MS Word document or similar program.

Functional vs. Chronological Resume

The Chronological resume is the most widely requested resume format by recruiters and hiring managers. If you send them a functional resume they will often send it back and ask for a chronological resume. Worse yet, they may reject your application and not contact you at all.

A functional resume is used by candidates seeking a complete career change. If you are simply taking transferrable skills from one product space to another, or seeking the next move up in your career path, the functional resume will not help you.

You may integrate some of the elements of a functional resume into your Professional Summary section, using more descriptions of transferable skills, and a bullet list or table, highlighting your areas of expertise.

Following your Professional Summary, and your Technical Skills section if you are using one, your Chronological Work History can easily highlight the transferrable skills (and successes) you wish to take forward into your new role. Simply utilize the STAR Method of Accomplishment Stories and develop the right bullets to achieve this.

This will satisfy the desires of the recruiters and hiring managers you are contacting. It will also help you direct future conversations toward the topics that will get you recognized as qualified and competent for each opportunity.

 *The STAR Career Workbook*

The Importance of the Professional Summary

As mentioned before, I do not recommend posting your professional objective at the top of your resume, but instead, launching into your Professional Summary (or Professional Introduction). The Professional Summary answers the question for the reader, "should I continue reading this resume?" Your goal is to capture the attention of the reader with an impactful overview of how you match their needs. If you have taken the time to work through the section on writing your Professional Introduction, then you are 90% done! If not, go back and do your homework!

See the Resume Format template on the following pages for how to integrate your Professional Introduction into your resume as your Professional Summary.

Options for the title your Professional Summary:

- Professional Summary
- Professional Introduction
- Professional Overview
- Executive Summary
- Executive Overview
- or – Your Title (i.e. Senior Software Engineer)

As to the last title recommendation, this is my favorite. It is very impactful to launch into your Professional Summary by using your professional title. **This may not be your actual current or past title, but rather, it could be the title you are pursuing.** Again, as with developing your Career Vision, I encourage you to think big here. Additionally, you may need to change out the title you use here for different jobs you pursue. You can even match the title of your Professional Summary to the title of the job posting which the company is using.

Example:

Senior Executive: Product and Service Leadership
Dynamic leadership career directing the successful design, development, implementation, and optimization of products, services, processes, and teams for technology startup, turnaround, and global expansion. Leveraged astute product development, marketing, and financial skills to create and grow sales, service, and customer support operations into multimillion dollar profit centers. Forward-thinking, change agent with exceptional results in managing multiple tasks, cross-group teams, client relationships, and projects simultaneously, to quickly address client needs and resolve customer and business problems.

Demonstrated accomplishments in:

- Product & Process Excellence
- Staff Development & Supervision
- Technical Innovation

Draft your Professional Summary now…

 *The STAR Career Workbook*

Driving Attention to your Successes Using STAR bullets

Evolving from a good resume, to a STAR resume, starts with integrating your STAR stories of key successes into your resume as bullet points under each job. In the Recommended Resume Format on the following pages, I recommend a minimum of 3 STAR bullets for each job listing, including multiple jobs under one employer. However, if you were in an assignment for only a short while, you might list only one or two bullet points.

The STAR bullet points are for accomplishments. Integrate your job duties and functions into the short description of your responsibilities. If the employer wants to know more about your day-to-day responsibilities, they will ask. It is more important to drive the conversation, and the eyes, to your successes. These are the things you accomplished, that helped the bottom line results of the organization.

I encourage you to always have some "hard number" result identified in each accomplishment. Sometimes this is really a "soft number," as in "created new revenue stream of approx. $6M annually, through introduction of new SaaS solution adapted from existing technical platform." The product or solution may have just launched. You may not have been fully informed of the first year's results. But you, as a key player in launching the product, should have an educated estimate.

The most difficult challenge in getting your STAR bullets incorporated into your resume should be the challenge of "boiling down" the STAR story into a 2 line bullet point. The key components of the **STAR** story, for the resume, are the **A**ction and **R**esults.

This will drive the conversation in the interview, to your STAR story. It will allow you to explain the **Situation** and the **Trial**, emphasizing the pain points, and barriers you faced to get the project completed.

Using STAR bullets also allows you to answer multiple behavioral-based questions using one STAR story. In your explanation of the bullet, you can include a variety of different issues you had to overcome, to get the project done. You may have been challenged with identifying resources, or you may have had to deal with various people issues. You may have had to troubleshoot past the work of others, or you may have faced complex technical challenges that required new learning on your part. Each of these challenges may surface, as separate behavioral questions, from good interviewers. You can use the same STAR bullet as a reference, to answer multiple challenges.

Example:
- Within 6 months, grew 15-person support team into 50-member support center in Seattle, providing 24X7 global support and service, while improving gross margins 19 points year over year to 46%.

The STAR bullet above was derived from a much larger story that this candidate is prepared to discuss. He is ready to discuss how he had to let a few long-time team members go, for past lack of performance, then re-grow the team to 50.

He is prepared to talk about how he had to negotiate some complex contracts with service providers, that had previously been gouging the organization on price-point. He is prepared to talk about how he had to align strategically, the handling of various large-sized and large-valued accounts, within the team, to insure the 46% results in the end.

> Driving the reader to the **a**ction and **r**esults leaves the opportunity to tell these stories in an interview!

If you have not done so already, go back **now** to your STAR Story Worksheets and convert your STAR Stories into boiled-down STAR Resume Bullets.

The STAR Career Workbook

Power Verbs

Use these power verbs to give impact to your resume. Come back to this chart whenever you are stuck searching for a good way to say something you have done.

A

abated	aligned	anticipated	calculated	cleared
abbreviated	allayed	appeased	calibrated	closed
abolished	alleviated	applied	capitalized	coached
abridged	allocated	appointed	captured	coded
absolved	allotted	appraised	cared for	collaborated
absorbed	altered	approached	carried	collated
accelerated	amassed	appropriated	carved	collected
accentuated	aroused	approved	categorized	combined
accommodated	arranged	arbitrated	catalogued	commanded
accomplished	articulated	amended	caught	commended
accounted for	ascertained	analyzed	cautioned	commenced
accrued	aspired	**B**	cemented	commissioned
accumulated	assembled	balanced	certified	communicated
achieved	assessed	began	chaired	compared
acquired	assigned	benchmarked	challenged	compiled
acted	assimilated	bid	championed	complemented
adapted	assisted	billed	changed	completed
adopted	assured	blended	charged	composed
added	attained	blocked	charted	compounded
addressed	attended	bolstered	checked	computed
adjusted	audited	boosted	connected	conceived
administered	augmented	bought	chose	concentrated
advanced	authored	branded	chronicled	conceptualized
advertised	authorized	bridged	circulated	condensed
advised	automated	broadened	circumvented	conducted
advocated	averted	brought	cited	conferred
affirmed	avoided	budgeted	clarified	configured
aided	awarded	built	classified	confirmed
alerted	answered		cleaned	confronted

Page | 82

Power Verbs (continued)

C (continued)	D			F
conserved	dealt	displayed	elicited	explored
considered	debated	disposed	eliminated	expressed
consolidated	debugged	disproved	embraced	extended
constructed	decided	dissected	emphasized	extracted
consulted	decoded	disseminated	empowered	**F**
consummated	decreased	dissolved	enabled	fabricated
contacted	dedicated	distinguished	encouraged	facilitated
continued	defined	distributed	ended	factored
contracted	delegated	diversified	enforced	familiarized
contributed	delineated	diverted	engaged	fielded
controlled	delivered	divested	engineered	filled
converted	derived	divided	enhanced	finalized
conveyed	described	documented	enlisted	financed
convinced	designated	doubled	enriched	fine tuned
cooperated	designed	drafted	enrolled	finished
coordinated	detailed	drew up	ensured	fixed
copied	detected	drove	entertained	focused
corrected	determined	demonstrated	enticed	forecasted
corresponded	developed	deployed	equipped	forged
counseled	devised	**E**	established	formalized
created	diagnosed	earned	estimated	formed
critiqued	differentiated	eased	evaluated	formulated
cultivated	diffused	economized	examined	fortified
customized	directed	edited	exceeded	forwarded
cut	disbursed	educated	executed	fostered
	discovered	effected	exercised	fought
	discussed	elaborated	expedited	found
	dispatched	elected	experimented	founded
	dispensed	elevated	explained	framed
				fulfilled

The STAR Career Workbook

Power Verbs (continued)

G	I	J	M	N
gained	identified	joined	made	named
garnered	ignited	judged	maintained	narrated
gathered	illustrated	justified	managed	navigated
gauged	implemented	**L**	mandated	negotiated
gave	imported	launched	maneuvered	netted
generated	improved	learned	manipulated	neutralized
governed	improvised	lectured	manufactured	nominated
graduated	included	led	mapped	normalized
grasped	incorporated	lessened	marked	notified
greeted	increased	leveraged	marketed	nurtured
grew	indicated	licensed	mastered	**O**
grouped	individualized	lifted	maximized	observed
guaranteed	indoctrinated	limited	measured	obtained
guided	induced	linked	mediated	offered
H	influenced	liquidated	memorized	officiated
halted	informed	listened	mentored	offset
halved	infused	litigated	merged	opened
handled	initiated	loaded	merited	operated
headed	innovated	located	met	optimized
heightened	inspected	logged	minimized	orchestrated
held	inspired		mobilized	ordered
helped	installed		modeled	organized
hired	instilled		moderated	oriented
honed	instituted		modified	originated
hosted	instructed		molded	outdistanced
hypnotized	insured		monitored	outlined
hypothesized	integrated		monopolized	outperformed
	intensified		motivated	overcame
	interacted		mounted	overhauled
			moved	oversaw
			multiplied	owned

Page | 84

The STAR Career Workbook

Power Verbs (continued)

P		R	
paced	procured	raised	remodeled
packaged	produced	rallied	rendered
packed	profiled	ranked	renegotiated
pared	programmed	rated	renewed
participated	progressed	reached	reorganized
partnered	projected	realigned	repaired
passed	promoted	realized	replaced
penetrated	proofread	rearranged	replicated
perceived	proposed	reasoned	reported
perfected	protected	rebuilt	represented
performed	proved	recognized	reproduced
persuaded	provided	recommended	requested
photographed	pruned	reconciled	researched
piloted	publicized	reconstructed	reserved
pinpointed	purchased	recorded	resolved
pioneered	pursued	recovered	restored
placed	Q	recruited	restructured
planned	quadrupled	rectified	retained
played	qualified	redesigned	retooled
praised	quantified	redirected	retrieved
predicted	queried	reduced	returned
prepared	questioned	re-engineered	revamped
prescribed	quoted	referred	reversed
presented		refocused	reviewed
preserved		registered	revised
presided		regulated	revitalized
prevailed		rehabilitated	revolutionized
prevented		reinforced	rewarded
printed		reiterated	risked
prioritized		released	rotated
processed		relieved	routed

The STAR Career Workbook

Power Verbs (continued)

T	U	V	W
tabulated	uncovered	validated	weathered
tackled	underlined	valued	weighed
talked	underscored	vaulted	widened
tallied	undertook	verbalized	withstood
targeted	underwrote	verified	won
tasted	unearthed	viewed	worked
taught	unified	visualized	wove
teamed	united	voiced	wrote
tempered	updated	volunteered	**Y**
tended	upgraded		yielded
terminated	upheld		
tested	urged		
testified	used		
tied	utilized		
took			
topped			
totaled			
traced			
tracked			
trained			
transcribed			
transformed			
transitioned			
translated			
transmitted			
traveled			
trimmed			
tripled			
troubleshot			
turned			
tutored			

The STAR Career Workbook

Recommended Resume Format

First Name Last Name
City (or metro area), State
Phone: (512) 555-1212
Email: first.last@xyz.com
www.linkedin.com/in/yourURL/

Professional Summary
This is a brief re-statement of your Professional Introduction, or elevator speech. You will strip out the first-person pronouns, reduce your use of **the** and **an,** and boil it down to about 4 lines. You may add a few bullet points underneath to emphasize some areas of expertise, or industries in which you've specialized.

- Area of Expertise #1
- Area of Expertise #2
- Area of Expertise #3
- Area of Expertise #4
- Area of Expertise #5
- Area of Expertise #6

Professional Experience
Company Name, City, State, Year to Year
Title
Brief description of company can be placed here, often done in italics.

Responsibilities: Brief overview of key responsibilities is placed here. Keep this overview to no more than two to three lines of text. Use short, no-pronoun sentences. Make some tough choices of what to keep.

Accomplishments:
- First bullet should reflect the achievement of which you are most proud, and that which reflects the function and role you want to pursue going forward.
- Your accomplishment bullets are derived from your STAR statements of key accomplishments, developed earlier in this

 ## The STAR Career Workbook

book, and give you ammunition for discussions during interviews and networking. Each job should have around 3 accomplishment bullets.

- Remember to work in hard number results that supported your company's bottom line (i.e. Achieved a 20% increase in new client engagement/retention... Reduced manufacturing cost by 5%, resulting in an estimated savings of $6M over 2 years.)

*Repeat **Professional Experience** for each job, going back approximately 10 years. This depends on how much you need to capture, breadth and depth of your career, and length of resume. I do not recommend exceeding 3 pages, and 2 pages is the optimal length.*

Military Experience (if any)
Rank on departure, Branch of Service, Last Station/Base location, City and State or Country. (Note: no years)

Responsibilities: (optional – as relevant to career and job search) Brief overview of key responsibilities are placed here. Keep this overview to no more than two lines of text. Use short, no-pronoun sentences. Make some tough choices of what to keep, and what to keep out.

Key Accomplishment:

- (Also optional - as relevant to career and job search). Pick one, or up to 3 military achievements of which you are most proud, and that which reflects the function and role you want to pursue going forward.

Technical Skills (for technology-focused applicants move to first page, just under Professional Summary – others keep at end, just before education).

This area is usually put together in a bullet or table format. It's not important to get every technology you've ever used in here, and you do not have to organize them perfectly into categories, but organization does help the eye-ball reader. See sample below, or in a sample

Technology Resume. Change the headings below as needed. Remove table borders or use very light borders. List all technologies in each category, separated by simple commas. The objective is to get the keywords in there, for easy-searching by recruiters and hiring managers.

> **Hardware/Operating Systems:**
> **Programming Languages:**
> **Software / Applications:**
> **Databases / CRM / ERP:**

Education & Certifications

Degree (in bold, using common abbreviation), Major Course of Study, University, City, State (or country). (Note: no years)

CERT (in bold, using common abbreviation), spell out Cert. name, Name of Cert. Organization, City/State where completed. (note: no years)

Awards & Associations

- Optional section. No penalty for not using it.
- Can also list Publications and Patents.
- Bullet list your key awards and professional associations.
- Keep your list brief and relevant to your career and future pursuits.

The STAR Career Workbook

Resume Worksheet

Take some time to fill in these blanks and see how your resume will flow.

Name and Contact Info

_____

_____

_____

Professional Summary

Technical Skills (optional – if not a technology-focused candidate, move to end of resume, before or after Education).

_____ :	
_____ :	
_____ :	
_____ :	

The STAR Career Workbook

Professional Experience

Company Name, City, State, Year to Year

_____

Responsibilities:

_____
_____
_____
_____

Accomplishments:

- _____
- _____
- _____
- _____
- _____

 *The STAR Career Workbook*

Professional Experience (continued)

Company Name, City, State, Year to Year

_____

Responsibilities:

_____
_____
_____
_____

Accomplishments:

- _____
- _____
- _____
- _____
- _____

The STAR Career Workbook

Professional Experience (continued)

Company Name, City, State, Year to Year

_____

Responsibilities:
_____
_____
_____
_____

Accomplishments:

- _____

- _____

- _____

- _____

- _____

The STAR Career Workbook

Military Experience (if any)
_____

Responsibilities:
_____
_____

Key Accomplishments:

- _____
- _____
- _____

Education & Certifications

- _____
- _____
- _____
- _____

Awards & Associations

- _____
- _____
- _____
- _____

The STAR Career Workbook

Resume QA

Take some time now to run a Quality Assurance Test on your Resume, using the checklist below. Return to this checklist often to make sure, as your document evolves and changes, that it meets with the standards you've decided are important, and with the "best practices" in the market today.

Quality Assurance Test Questions	Yes / No + Solution
Does your resume reflect your professional objective? Is it consistent with the types of jobs you are pursuing, and the career path you wish to pursue?	
Does your resume speak the language of your industry, using the terms and terminology of an expert in your field, while also not using too much jargon as to confuse someone not in your field?	
Does your resume show that you have the knowledge of your industry, required to manage the issues you will face, problems that you will solve, and solutions that you will develop, in the roles you are pursuing?	
Will your resume appeal to a decision maker in an organization where you want to work? Will it make that person want to meet you and talk to you?	
Are your professional introduction / summary concise and focused? Is the language specific, and focused on the target employers you wish to pursue?	

The STAR Career Workbook

Quality Assurance Test Questions	Yes / No + Solution
Is your title accurately conveyed, at the level of experience you've attained, and in language that both industry insiders and outsiders can understand?	
Do your professional introduction / summary clearly outline your areas of expertise, years of experience, and level of responsibility you've held?	
Are your professional introduction / summary strong and convincing, exciting and compelling? Do you enjoy reading it? Are others inspired by reading it?	
Does your job history / experience section reflect a career progression vs. a career plateau or a backwards movement?	
Does each of your accomplishment bullets reflect a specific action, followed by a result, that benefitted the organization?	

The STAR Career Workbook

Quality Assurance Test Questions	Yes / No + Solution
Do the results in your accomplishment bullets provide measurable **hard numbers** whenever possible? Have you conveyed the bottom-line contribution to the employer in each accomplishment?	
Is your level of involvement in obtaining the results clearly identified in each accomplishment bullet?	
Do your accomplishment bullets reflect the language of your field, and the areas of highest need in your industry?	
Are your accomplishment bullets no more than four lines in length (preferably 2 - 3)?	
Does the information about your education, training, awards, and memberships in professional associations, support your objective? Is it focused on your target market and its needs?	
Does the information about your education, training, awards, and memberships in professional associations, add to your credibility, increase the likelihood of you getting an interview, and show the potential for a direct contribution to your past and future employers?	

 *The STAR Career Workbook*

STAR Cover Letters, References and Referrals

Cover Letters

Cover letters can be a powerful tool to help you get attention from a hiring manager, or at the least, moved past the gatekeeper into the hiring manager's hands. You also run the risk of seeing your work of art ignored or scoffed at, and your candidacy declined before your resume is reviewed. That's not to say that you would NOT include a cover letter. In almost all cases of applying for a job, or sending your resume to a contact, you will want to include a cover letter. What you say and how you say it is the key.

The purpose of the cover letter is to help the reader understand clearly that you are a candidate they would want to move along in the process.

Special Note:

When you have been given a name of a decision maker, make sure the first sentence connects the person who referred you. If emailing, cc the person who referred you.

1. Do not attach your resume. Wait for it to be requested.
2. Ask for something, or you'll get nothing … a meeting, another introduction, a reply with feedback.
3. Promise to follow up within a specified time, and then do it!

The STAR Career Workbook

Introduction Letters

Introduction Letters are used to generate leads and **get your foot in the door** at a company where you hope to uncover a hidden job opportunity. You may work with this employer to create a position tailored to your unique value.

The components/paragraphs are the content from your marketing plan, flowing from…
- (1) Moving Forward Statement, to
- (2) Professional Introduction, and then to
- (3) Professional Objective.
- (4) You would then tie in some knowledge you have gained from researching the company, and use a STAR accomplishment story to show how you have addressed a similar issue.

Use the worksheet on the following page to draft an Introduction Letter to your #1 target employer. You will likely modify this slightly, for each different company or contact to which you send it.

You might send an Introduction Letter in many different mediums, through email, online communications, and by direct mail. Be sure that the introduction letter is addressed to a real person, and that you have the correct spelling of the name of the person you are addressing.

The STAR Career Workbook

Introduction Letter Worksheet

Your Name and Contact Info

Dear _____ (get a name, refer to a person),

I was referred to you / I am contacting you to explore an employment opportunity at _____ (company name). After researching your organization, I find consistency with my core values of _____, _____ and _____, and I would love to join your team!

I am a (Professional Summary)

Some key accomplishments of mine, that appear directly relevant to your current situation include (list 2 or 3 in paragraph or bullet form).

 **The STAR Career Workbook**

I am focused on (Professional Objective)

```
┌─────────────────────────────────────────┐
│                                         │
│                                         │
│                                         │
└─────────────────────────────────────────┘
```

and I believe that your company has a match for that objective.

Please consider me for current open roles, and also for roles still being conceived at your company. If my experiences open ideas of any kind, for ways I can help further your goals, I welcome the opportunity to discuss this.

I will follow up with you within 3 business days to schedule a time to meet you, on the phone or in person, regarding this opportunity.

I look forward to speaking with you then!

Sincerely,

_____
Signature

_____
Printed Full Name

# The STAR Career Workbook

Job-Ad-Response cover letter

If you are applying for a specific job opportunity, the approach is different. The gatekeeper has a checklist of requirements that all candidates must pass, and he or she wishes to know quickly, if you pass the list. MOST of that checklist can be found in the job posting, so the **Job-Ad-Response Cover Letter** would answer, item-by-item, how your knowledge, skills, and abilities match those of the posted job opening.

DO NOT focus exclusively on the list of "job requirements"; also look at the job duties and job scope for items you should also address. If the list is extensive, I recommend you use bullet points to draw the eye to each item.

If the job posting is vague, or not very detailed in its list of requirements, then address what you can from their posting, and shift back to your Moving Forward Statement, Professional Introduction, and one or two STAR accomplishment stories.

I recommend a cover letter of no more than 4 paragraphs, and preferably 3. Wrap up your cover letter with a very positive outlook, a pre-closing kind of statement like, "I look forward to meeting you in person, so we can go over this opportunity in more detail."

Use the worksheet on the following pages to draft a **Job-Ad-Response Cover Letter,** to another target employer with a current posting you are qualified for. You will modify this slightly, for each different job ad you respond to.

The STAR Career Workbook

Job-Ad-Response Cover Letter Worksheet

Your Name and Contact Info

Dear _____ (get a name, and refer to a person if possible, or address it to "Hiring Manager"),

I am excited to put my name forward for the role of _____ (job posting title, with reference number, if provided) at _____ (company name).

I am a (Professional Summary)

I am focused on (Professional Objective)

and I believe this role is a match for that objective.

Below is an overview of how my skills and experiences align with this opportunity:

Requirement: (address at least the top 5)	My Skills or Experience (years with this skill and your aptitude (i.e. highly skilled).
• Product Management:	10+ years, highly skilled, successful launch of over 20 new products.

The STAR Career Workbook

In addition, my career has afforded me the following accomplishments, which appear directly relevant to the challenges in this role: (list 2 or 3 STAR bullets).

Please consider me for this job posting, for any other current open roles, and also for roles still being conceived at your company.

If my experiences open ideas of any kind, for ways I can help further your goals, I welcome the opportunity to discuss this further.

I will follow up with you within 3 business days to schedule a time to meet you, on the phone or in person, regarding this opportunity. I look forward to speaking with you then!

Sincerely,

_____
Signature

_____
Printed Full Name

The STAR Career Workbook

Recommendation Letters

I do recommend that you gather recommendation letters. The process of doing this will help you build confidence, refine your message, and make possible contacts for job leads. The earlier you get started with this process, the more effective it can be for you. There are two key ways to gather recommendations.

First, you can use the LinkedIn feature of requesting recommendations from your colleagues. Other social media sites have similar features. Use them all. For LinkedIn, go to edit your profile, and scroll down to the 'Recommendations' area. Hover your mouse over the area near the top, and you should see **Ask to be recommended**. First, choose the role for which you are seeking a recommendation, and then search your connections for a colleague from that company. Make sure that you personalize the request, and see below for additional guidance. *(Note: LinkedIn, and other sites, regularly rearrange how these features are used, so please excuse me if my specific instructions don't match with the current structure).*

I also recommend that you reach out directly to colleagues, and ask for an email or document that would include a similar recommendation. You can essentially hand a script to your contact. Tell them exactly what you'd like them to say, citing a specific STAR story that connects you, and/or your professional strengths you'd like them to highlight. The Recommendation Letter Request Worksheet on the following pages will help you with this.

When someone has written a recommendation letter for you, ALWAYS write a reciprocal recommendation, whenever possible and appropriate.

 *The STAR Career Workbook*

Who should you get recommendations from? *Jot down some names that come to mind:*

- Most recent manager:
  _____

- Most recent co-worker:
  _____

- Most recent direct-report:
  _____

- Past managers:
  _____
  _____

- Customers / clients:
  _____
  _____

- Vendors:
  _____
  _____

The STAR Career Workbook

When should you give your recommendation letters to your networking contacts, recruiters or hiring managers?

You will send or attach a recommendation letter (or you may paste a link to your LinkedIn page where the recommendation lives), when you are asking your contact at a potential employer, to move you to the next step.

For example:

> "John,
>
> Thank you for your attention to the following information about my qualifications and objectives. I have attached 2 recommendation letters I have recently received; one from a past manager and one from a co-worker.
>
> I need your assistance in getting this information into the hands of Bob Jones, your VP of Development. Please include a cover note with any recommendation you are also willing to give me.
>
> After you are able to send this to him, I'd like to visit you at your offices and see if you could introduce me personally to Bob.
>
> Please confirm when you have sent this over to Bob and I will call you to schedule that next step."

The STAR Career Workbook

Recommendation Letter Request Worksheet

Dear _____,

I am writing to request some very important support from you. I hope to reciprocate as soon as possible. I'd like to ask you for a recommendation letter which addresses some key successes I had when we worked together at _____ (company name).

As you know, I am a (Professional Summary)

[   ]

I am focused on (Professional Objective)

[   ]

During my tenure at _____ (company name), I was successful with the following key accomplishment(s), and I would like you to reference this / these experience(s) in your recommendation letter.
(List 1 or 2 STAR bullets)

[   ]

The STAR Career Workbook

Would you please email back to me with a recommendation letter? You can attach it as a separate document or just send it in the body of an email. I will be able to forward this on to key contacts I am making during my job search.

(or)

Would you please write a recommendation for me on LinkedIn (or other social media site)? Here is a link to my profile: [Insert URL to your LinkedIn Profile]. I will be able to forward this on to key contacts I am making during my job search.

Thank you so much for considering this request, and please let me know if there is any way I can assist you with anything. I will be very happy to support you.

Sincerely,

Printed Full Name
Email Address
Phone Number
LinkedIn URL

 **The STAR Career Workbook**

References

Your reference people need to be prepared to take a call or email, and respond to a variety of questions (see example below) about your skills and experience, personality, and style. Some of the individuals who write a recommendation letter for you may also serve as references, but some will not.

I recommend that you contact the individuals whom you wish to list as references, NOW. Speak to them at length about your situation and your plans. Have the following ready to discuss, and don't hesitate to send them drafts:

1. Exit/Moving Forward Statement
2. Elevator Pitch / Positioning Statement
3. Professional Summary / Introduction
4. Professional Objective and
5. STAR stories

Tell your references exactly what you'd like them to say when they are called, including the professional strengths you'd like them to highlight, and a specific STAR story (or two) that connects you.

Tell your references the target companies where you are applying and pursuing leads, so that they can be prepared for preliminary contact by insiders in those companies ("unofficial" reference checks).

When you are asked to provide your references, perhaps after an interview or screening on a job opportunity, immediately notify your reference people, so that they can be prepared for contact.

Keep your references informed of your status, any leads you are following, interviews you have had, and names of contact people who you've met (people who might call them).

The STAR Career Workbook

References List Worksheet

1. Most recent manager or supervisor

Name	
Phone #	
Email Address	

2. Second most recent manager or supervisor

Name	
Phone #	
Email Address	

3. A peer from your most recent or previous job

Name	
Phone #	
Email Address	

4. An internal or external client from most recent or previous job

Name	
Phone #	
Email Address	

5. Someone who reported to you (or you mentored/trained)

Name	
Phone #	
Email Address	

# The STAR Career Workbook

Sample Reference Check

Following is a Sample Reference Check that might be done by a recruiter, third party or hiring manager. What would your chosen references say about you when asked these questions? What do you **WANT** them to say?

1. What was your professional relationship to _____?

2. How long have you known _____?

3. What job did he/she perform?

4. What can you tell me about _____'s knowledge and performance in this position?

5. In your opinion, what are his/her three most important strengths?
    1.
    2.
    3.

6. What were his/her key achievements while reporting to you, working with you, or supporting your objectives?
    1.
    2.
    3.

7. What would be an area you feel _____ could improve/develop in his/her career?

8. If an appropriate position were available within your organization, would you recommend _____ for hire or re-hire?

The STAR Career Workbook

Job Applications

You will have a number of occasions where you might need to complete a standardized application form, particularly if you are applying for government, military, or university jobs. You will also need to complete a profile when you are applying to jobs on a corporate careers website.

On the next page you will find a sample standardized form. Take some time now to enter your information, so that you know how you will respond consistently on job applications going forward.

In all cases, with regard to job application forms, you should follow and understand these things:

- Be Brief.
- Refer to your resume where possible.
- Details in the job application should match your resume.
- While your resume will not specify dates in some cases (such as your year of high school diploma), some applications may require this information.
- The full job application is rarely reviewed for professional, private sector jobs, but is often used for government jobs.
- Every piece of data is not required. Watch for indications of what items are required, and concentrate on getting those completed.
- Be careful to record the same dates you have in your resume. If dates are optional on education, military years, etc., do not provide them.
- Save copies of your government and university applications so that you can re-use them on multiple opportunities.

The STAR Career Workbook

Master Job Application Template

Take time now to fill in this blank employment application form, so you know what information you'll need to provide when applying for a job.

Applicant Information:

Applicant Name	
Home Phone	
Mobile Phone	
Email Address	

Address	
City	
State	
Zip	

Are you applying for?

Temporary work	[ ] Y or [ ] N
Part-time work?	[ ] Y or [ ] N
Full-time work?	[ ] Y or [ ] N
When can you start?	
Can you work weekends?	[ ] Y or [ ] N
Can you work evenings?	[ ] Y or [ ] N
Can you work overtime?	[ ] Y or [ ] N
Salary desired:	$_____

Personal Information:

Do you have transportation to/from work?	[ ] Y or [ ] N
Are you over the age of 18?	[ ] Y or [ ] N
Can you present evidence of your work eligibility in the United States?	[ ] Y or [ ] N

The STAR Career Workbook

If hired, are you willing to submit to, and pass, a controlled substance (drug) test?	[ ] Y or [ ] N
In compliance with federal law, all persons hired will be required to verify identity and eligibility to work in the United States, and to complete the required employment eligibility verification form upon hire. Please initial that you understand this requirement.	_____ Your Initials
Are you able to perform the essential functions of the job for which you are applying, with or without reasonable accommodation?	[ ] Y or [ ] N
If no, describe the functions that cannot be performed	

(Note: We will comply with the ADA and consider reasonable accommodation measures that may be necessary for eligible applicants/employees to perform essential functions.)

Have you ever been convicted of a criminal offense (felony only)?	[ ] Y or [ ] N
If yes, please describe the crime(s), when and where convicted, and disposition of the case.	

(Note: No applicant will be denied employment solely on the grounds of conviction of a criminal offense. The date of the offense, the nature of the offense, including any significant details that affect the description of the event, and the surrounding circumstances and the relevance of the offense to the position(s) applied for may be considered.)

Education, Training, and Experience:

For this section, you will want to match your application content to the content in your resume, as closely as you can. Your resume will likely not include dates of when you completed early phases of your education, but the employment application may require dates. If it is required, provide it.

 *The STAR Career Workbook*

Employment History:
For this section, you will want to match your application content to the content in your resume, as closely as you can. Your resume will likely have dates for each of your job listings in your employment history, including promotions at each employer. Make sure those dates are consistent with what you put in your employment applications.

References:
As you have previously completed data for a Reference List, you should have this ready for an employment application, should it be required.

Standard Certifications:
You will be asked to sign the application, attesting to some, or all, of the following types of statements…

I certify that I have not purposely withheld any information that might adversely affect my chances for hiring. I attest to the fact that the answers given by me are true & correct to the best of my knowledge and ability. I understand that any omission (including any misstatement) of material fact on this application, or on any document used to secure employment, can be grounds for rejection of application or, if I am employed by this company, terms for my immediate termination of employment with the company.

I understand that if I am employed, my employment is not definite, and can be terminated at any time, either with or without prior notice, and by either me or the company. (At-Will Employment Clause)

I permit the company to examine my references, record of employment, education record, and any other information I have provided. I authorize the references I have listed, to disclose any information related to my work record and my professional experiences with them, without giving me prior notice of such disclosure. In addition, I release the company, my former employers, and all other persons, corporations, partnerships, and associations, from any and all claims, demands, or liabilities, arising out of, or in any way related to, such examination or revelation.

The STAR Career Workbook

STAR Networking

Networking Basics

Now that you have prepared your marketing materials (resume, cover letters, references, and interview preparation materials), and you have your communication strategy aligned, it is time to tackle your Networking Strategy. You will recall that the STAR methodology emphasizes networking, and targeting specific employers, for your next career opportunity. This is hard work, and there are many gatekeepers and potential dead ends. "Be strong and courageous. Do not be afraid; do not be discouraged, for the LORD your God will be with you wherever you go." Joshua 1:9

To have this confidence, it is important to have a solid foundation in Networking Basics.

Networking begins with building a broad base of contacts, with all persons you know and should know. All contacts are valuable. All contacts have the potential to lead you to other contacts, within your target companies. You **will** be surprised to learn who else your many contacts know, and who they will meet.

The worksheets in this chapter, will guide you in identifying a starting base of contacts. You will want to build this base further and further, to broaden your prospects for identifying key contacts.

The networking process can be viewed as building a basic 3D block pyramid. It begins with a solid foundation of your many contacts; friends, family, co-workers, customers, local business contacts, and professional association acquaintances. It builds to contacts within target organizations, and increases in levels toward top decision-makers at your target employers.

 *The STAR Career Workbook*

Within your base of contacts, you will identify where they are working and have worked, what level of decision-making they have in their organizations, and ideally who they know and can introduce you to, within your target companies.

The networking pyramid begins with a base level of a diverse set of people you know, former bosses, co-workers, neighbors, old college friends, neighbors, church friends, people you know through hobbies, the real estate agent who sold you your home, etc.

When you communicate your "message" about your current job search and goals, and <u>ask for their help</u>, they should introduce you to contacts they know at companies where you may have opportunities. You can also provide them with a short list of companies where you need contacts, and with a sample script of how they might introduce you. This helps them connect you further, with someone who can help advance your search.

The contacts you will meet at the **next** level will not know you well, but you will have a warm introduction. Your job then is to cultivate that relationship, learn from the new contact, and provide some value in advance to this person. Can you offer a lead to this person, that will help them in their current job, introduce them to someone you have met through your networking, or connect them with a volunteer opportunity, or hobby-group, in which they have an interest? You must cultivate that relationship enough (and this is a judgment call, but must be done rapidly during an active job search), before you ask them to introduce you further into their organization.

Ideally, your contact will introduce you to a hiring manager or decision maker in theirs, or another target company. My personal experience and observations reveal that the most meaningful results of networking (i.e. a sale, a job opportunity, a new business opportunity) happen at the 3rd level of networking. If your next introduction is to a hiring manager or decision maker, you are close to achieving this goal.

The STAR Career Workbook

The illustration below shows the building blocks of this process, and carries it through to your ultimate goal in the Career Networking process.

My personal experience in sales, recruiting, and networking, is that I will get 1 yes for every 6 or 7 requests. So, if I am looking for that elusive dream job, it may take as many as 7 of these pyramid climbs to reach that goal.

On the next page is a blank pyramid. You can use this tool in a number of ways.

1. Make a few copies so you can re-use it, or at least use a pencil if you are writing on it here in this workbook.

2. As a planning tool, to get a dream job in a target company, start at the top and chart backwards, to the various contacts you need to make.

3. As a tool to chart out your progress with an uncovered opportunity, start from the bottom, using the sample data you see to the right.

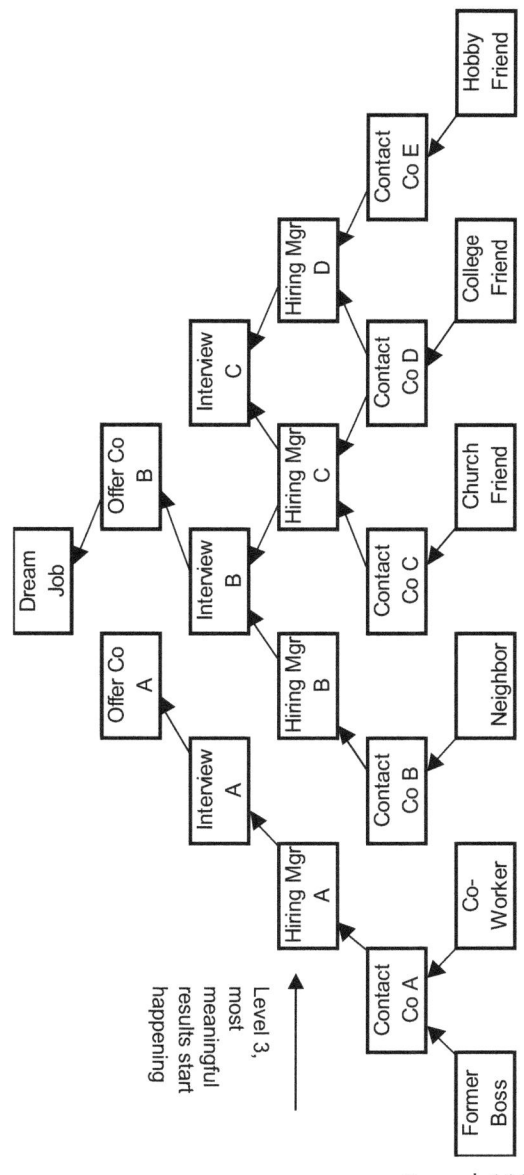

The STAR Career Workbook

Networking Pyramid

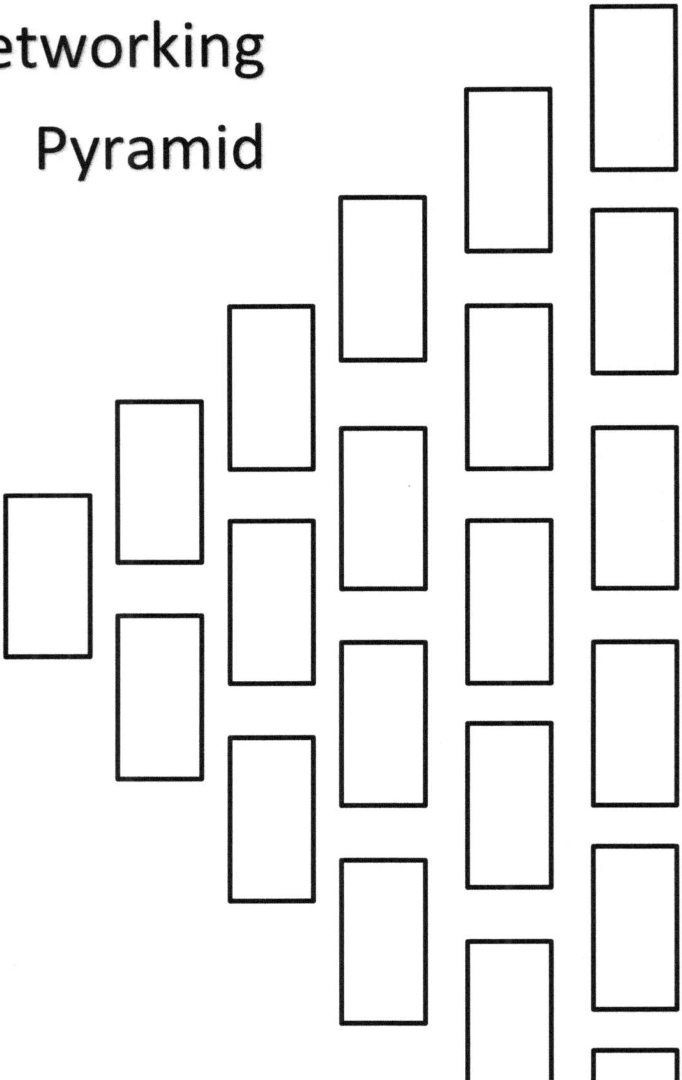

The STAR Career Workbook

Making your Network **Work!**

Your contacts are overworked, too busy for you, and have other things to do with their time. Like all humans, they are naturally self-centered and, selfish as well. HOWEVER... in the process of understanding their most pressing needs, you can offer some immediate, or long-term win-win contribution, in exchange for their help.

That contribution might simply be that by acquiring your talent in their company, their organization will improve, and everyone's lives will improve. It might be something more tangible, such as your efforts to introduce that contact to a person, or organization, that will benefit their career.

In some cases, you will have nothing to offer, and you should not be disheartened when a contact simply falls through on you, in your efforts to connect higher in his or her organization.

Using the sales funnel concept, realize that the more contacts you put in the funnel at the top, and the wider the spout is with additional contacts you develop, the better the chance you will see results at the end of the pipe.

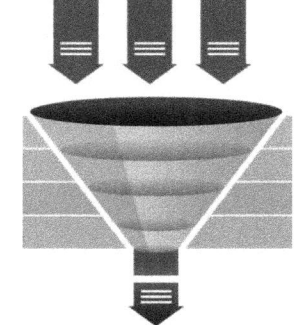

When you get your contacts working for your best interest, it is very important that they know what you need them to do!

Communicate regularly with your contacts using your:
1. Moving Forward Statement,
2. Professional Introduction, and
3. Professional Objective

The STAR Career Workbook

Build Your Support Network

Your support network starts with a foundation of FRIENDS AND FAMILY. These contacts will provide you with a safe space to release your emotions: anger, frustration, sadness, and depression. They will also encourage you, celebrate with you, and hold you accountable to your goals. Your Friends and Family network is also the FIRST place you will start networking for job leads.

TAKE SOME TIME NOW to write down the names of people you know. Later, go back to these lists, and work through them, to gather contact information for all of your contacts. Mark a star next to the contacts you need to touch base with, right now, for support.

Worksheets follow to start documenting your network. This is just the beginning, and eventually you will have so many contacts that the data could not possibly fit on these pages. Get started on it NOW!

RELATIVES		FRIENDS	
NAME	CONTACT INFO	NAME	CONTACT INFO

The STAR Career Workbook

NEIGHBORS		CHURCH/SYNAGOGUE	
NAME	CONTACT INFO	NAME	CONTACT INFO

ALUMNI		COMMUNITY	
NAME	CONTACT INFO	NAME	CONTACT INFO

 *The STAR Career Workbook*

SPORTS/HOBBIES		PERSONAL BUSINESS	
NAME	CONTACT INFO	NAME	CONTACT INFO

Build Your Professional Network

Your support network continues with business colleagues and contacts. These contacts should be treated with pure professionalism, and your request for job leads should be **rapid**.

TAKE SOME TIME NOW to write down the names of people you know. Later, go back to these lists and work through them, to gather contact information for all of your contacts. Mark a star next to the contacts you need to touch base with, right now, for support.

Fill in the worksheets on the following pages, for your Professional Network.

The STAR Career Workbook

PRESENT/ MOST RECENT CO-WORKERS		PRESENT / MOST RECENT MANAGERS	
NAME	CONTACT INFO	NAME	CONTACT INFO

PAST CO-WORKERS		PAST BOSSES	
NAME	CONTACT INFO	NAME	CONTACT INFO

The STAR Career Workbook

CUSTOMERS / VENDORS / SUPPLIERS		MENTORS, LEADERS, INSPIRERS	
NAME	CONTACT INFO	NAME	CONTACT INFO

PROFESSIONAL ASSOCIATION CONTACTS		CONTACTS FROM RECENT TRAINING/EDUCATION	
NAME	CONTACT INFO	NAME	CONTACT INFO

The STAR Career Workbook

Networking Meetings

To turn contacts into meetings, and those meetings into further introductions, you will need a battle plan for how you conduct yourself in your networking meetings. Following is a good agenda for your networking meetings. This agenda can be completed in minutes, or stretch for an hour over coffee or lunch.

- **S**et expectations: Let your contact know your goals for the meeting up front, but be clear that you wish the relationship to be win-win. Be prepared with something to offer your contact in advance of his/her assistance. For example, you might bring a lead that will help them in their current job, an introduction to someone who can help their career, or a connection with a group in which they have an interest.

- **T**alk about your search: Using your Exit/Moving Forward Statement, Professional Introduction, and Career Vision, discuss your search, target employers, and networking plans, with your contact. Be detailed and specific; don't leave them guessing about your direction.

- **A**sk for intelligence on the company where he/she works (or companies in which your contact has knowledge). Ask about the culture of the organization, pains and problems for the business, and the future of the organization.

- **R**eferrals: Ask for an introduction to hiring managers or decision-makers who can interview you for a real or potential job opportunity.

Once your contacts introduce you to a higher level contact, seek to connect with, and possibly meet this next-level contact. Your goal is to **UNDERSTAND** their needs, within their teams and organization, so that the strengths you will position, and the successes you will share, address their most pressing needs.

Next, you will leverage this opportunity to **PERSUADE** that person to champion your efforts to gain a foothold in their organization, using your Professional Introduction and STAR stories.

Finally, you will **ASK** this contact for a referral to the top decision-maker, who can offer you a position at their company.

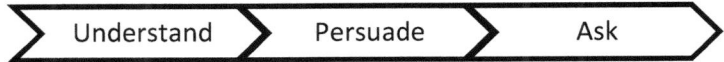

Career Search / Networking Goals

As I've shared with you before, career networking is a lot like sales. I use the "funnel" idea to illustrate that the more initial contacts, meetings, and connections you make, at the top of the funnel, the better will be your chances for closing a deal at the bottom.

I've got some pretty bold goals for you to consider, for the number of contacts you need to make, meetings you need to set up and opportunities you should be tracking, to land a good new job in a reasonable amount of time. I offer the following Career Search Productivity Tracker to illustrate these goals. You can take this same format and set it up in Microsoft Excel, or a similar spreadsheet program, then track your own results against the goals you decide are right for you. Note that my tracker provides a field for both the average number, as well as total number of events for each item. Keeping track of your averages helps to encourage you when your activity might taper off. At least you will know that you are tracking with the averages you need to uphold, to keep your search productive.

The STAR Career Workbook

Career Search Productivity Tracker

RESULTS Week Of:	Unique Networking Contacts	Hiring Manager Contacts	Job Applications	Hidden Opportunity Leads	Networking Meetings	Hiring Manager Meetings	Real Job Interviews		Average	Total
	50	5	5	5	3	3	1			

The STAR Career Workbook

Networking through Professional Associations

You are probably already a member of at least one professional organization related to your career path. If it is possible to engage with one or two more during this time, without incurring substantial cost, it is a good investment of time and resources. Many groups offer the ability to meet, without having to join right away, as a way to check them out.

These groups, and their meetings, offer great opportunities to meet other professionals in your field, and expand your contacts. You may not meet a potential hiring manager, but you will meet people who work at your target companies, and others who work at companies you should add to your target list. You will then get their business card, connect with them later online, research to see who they are connected to, and follow their connections toward hiring decision-makers.

Professional groups will usually have their own website, email distribution group, and job board or job leads list. Monitor these regularly, and follow up. But remember that these leads are just like any other job posting. You still have to make the contacts, and get the referrals and recommendations, to stand out from among the many other applicants.

Networking at local Job Search Clubs

Most metropolitan areas today have one or more prominent job search clubs or meetups. These are often non-profit organizations. Membership is typically free. The exposure, support, and training is phenomenal. Even most rural areas have a state-run workforce development and unemployment support center. You may be required to check in with one of these centers to claim unemployment insurance

# The STAR Career Workbook

benefits. Don't leave too quickly! Check out the many FREE resources, meetings, and services they provide.

I am very encouraged by the trend of seeing churches, synagogues, and mosques sponsoring job seeker groups. God's Words tell us that working hard; keeping faith in mind, can lead us to the great things He has planned for us.

Run a web search in your community, and find a group that meets at a time and location which is convenient and inspiring. Attend EVERY regular meeting. Make this a discipline. Sign up for free resume reviews, mock interviews, accountability groups, and coaching sessions.

Job Seeker/Job Search Clubs should feel welcoming, align to your values, have professional, relevant content, and quickly turn you toward actionable job leads. Otherwise, find another group.

Networking through Training and Education

If you are currently in, or have recently been through, a degree or training program, you probably connected with a number of people with whom you got along and enjoyed company. During a career search, it is even more important to connect with as many fellow students and alumni as possible; and like the leads you get from professional associations, follow their connections toward hiring decision-makers.

Look around you in the training programs or classes you are attending. Who do you "connect" with? Talk to them about your search, and find mutual ways you can support each other. Are you involved in any group projects or teams? Make sure you get to know your group and let them know you are job hunting. Remember to look for ways you can "pay forward" any help they might give you.

LinkedIn will show you people in your network, and within 1 or 2 levels away, who also attended your prep school, college, or university. Some of these contacts may be years away from you, and you may have nothing much in common, however, if you hail from a smaller school, or the other person was at least a few years within your range of years at the school, this is a warm lead – a helpful reference, to ask for a connection, and possible leads.

Networking through Happy Hours, Trade Shows and Conferences

You can spend a lot of time attending Happy Hours, networking events, and related social activities. You will also spend a lot of precious severance or savings dollars in the process. Be cognizant of the results you need from these events, and if you are not getting those results, then back off and regroup. Free events are great, and drinking a water cocktail helps as well. But your time is valuable, and these events often infringe on family and personal time. I recommend no more than 2 per week.

Conferences and Tradeshows are an excellent means of building contacts and finding leads. You can find creative ways to get in free, or at least with a discount. If you must pay a sizeable admission fee, analyze the potential impact of the event from the context of the pure number of quality contacts you are likely to make, rather than the pure interest you have in the topics, products, etc. Don't expect long conversations, in fact, avoid them. Meet and speak to as many good contacts as you can, get their business card, connect with them later online, research to see who they are connected to, and follow their connections toward hiring decision makers.

The STAR Career Workbook

Networking Events Planner

Professional Associations

Organization	Key Meetings	Dates	Cost

Local Job Search Clubs and Organizations

Organization	Key Meetings	Dates	Cost

Training and Education

Class	Audience Type	Dates	Cost

Happy Hours / Business Networking Events

Event	Target Audience	Dates	Cost

Trade Shows and Conferences

Event	Target Audience	Dates	Cost

 **The STAR Career Workbook**

Building Your Personal Brand

Your personal brand is your reputation in the marketplace. It is what people say about you when they describe you to other professionals.

As Laura Lake put it, "We all can be a brand and cultivate our power to stand out and be unique... Your personal brand should be about who you are and what you have to offer." Your personal brand, she says, "is the secret sauce that can make you stand out [in] a stack of resumes." (see https://www.thebalancesmb.com/creating-and-growing-personal-brand-2295814)

Joseph Liu adds, "Personal branding is a way of establishing and consistently reinforcing who you are and what you stand for in your career and life. Everything you do either strengthens or dilutes the personal brand you're trying to create." Joseph shared a tough reminder that, "If no one else... knows about my work accomplishments, those accomplishments won't really count for much." (see https://www.forbes.com/sites/josephliu/2018/04/30/personal-brand-work/#2ec9fc7b7232)

You want people in your network talking about the areas in which you are an expert, and the many positive outcomes you have created for the companies where you've worked. You get this discussion happening through your networking meetings, as previously discussed, and through your online connections and activity, **as you are about to review.**

You have already worked on the building blocks of your personal brand!

1. Exit/Moving Forward statement
2. Elevator Pitch / Positioning Statement
3. Professional Summary / Introduction
4. Professional Objective / Career Vision
5. Resume
6. STAR stories

 *The STAR Career Workbook*

Remember that in building these marketing materials, you also did exhaustive work to identify your core **strengths, values, and virtues**. These must be communicated through your personal brand as well.

The key to having a strong personal brand is active involvement in networking among your professional community, and **sharing your knowledge, expertise, and experiences**. This can be done in-person or virtually (online), but it must be:
- "On message" with your Professional Introduction and Professional Objective

- Relevant, polite, and helpful to the community where it is delivered or posted.

You have already identified who your TARGET AUDIENCE is for your personal branding efforts too! Go back and look at the notes you have taken for the many contacts you will network with. Take a look at the various notes you also took, for the various groups and activities through which you plan to network. This is your target audience.

For offline branding consider this short list of possible activities:
1. Volunteer to teach a class, give a presentation or deliver a training, either for a fee or for free, at an upcoming professional association meeting.
2. Offer consulting services, either for a fee or for free, to small businesses, start-ups, incubators, and the like, to "pass on" the expert skills you have developed in your larger corporate experiences.
3. Offer executive coaching to a leader trying to get a "break-through" at his or her company; or mentoring to a person who is "up-and-coming" in your industry.

Each time you confirm and complete each of these activities, make sure your community is aware that you are doing it through online and offline communications.

It's really that simple.

 *The STAR Career Workbook*

In the next section of this workbook, you are going to dive deeper into the use of social media and online networking, including how to build your various social media profiles, and how to engage with your online community.

You will also look at the possibility of developing a personal web page and/or blog, through which you can continue to expand on your core areas of expertise, and your strengths.

For a very detailed (they call it the "complete") guide to what else you might consider doing in your personal branding efforts, consider this online tutorial: https://www.quicksprout.com/the-complete-guide-to-building-your-personal-brand/

A word of caution:
The reason you picked up this workbook is because you are looking for a new or better job. You can spend so much time working on your personal brand that you lose sight of this goal. Also, companies that might consider hiring you, may lose sight of you. Make sure you stay focused on the task at hand.

Social Media and Online Networking

Your professional network of trusted contacts gives you an advantage in your career, and is one of your most valuable assets. In a globally connected economy, your success as a professional, and your competitiveness as a company, depends upon faster access to insight and resources you can trust. – *from LinkedIn*

In this section, I will review the various sites you should consider for your networking strategy, give you guidance on how best to use them, and offer some worksheets to help you plan your strategy.

 **LinkedIn (www.linkedin.com) is** probably the most influential and heavily used social networking site for business professionals. LinkedIn is an interconnected network of experienced professionals from around the world, representing hundreds of industries, and virtually every country on the planet. You can find, be introduced to, and collaborate with qualified professionals who can help you accomplish your goals. LinkedIn is absolutely essential in your career networking strategy.

Facebook. In the past, I did not recommend using Facebook for career networking. I only made exceptions for marketing, sales, and PR professionals. My position on this has changed. I now see Facebook as an excellent resource to connect with family, friends, past and present co-workers, and many contacts in many industries, to learn about new job opportunities. Companies, including mine are using Facebook to promote their employer brand, and to post job updates.

The STAR Career Workbook

 Twitter is a social networking and microblogging service utilizing instant messaging, SMS, or a web interface. Twitter is open-ended, and people and companies use it in a variety of ways, including to job search. Users post updates on Twitter that are displayed on the user's profile page, and delivered to other users who have signed up to receive them. Companies and job boards post job openings on Twitter, and job seekers network through Twitter to help facilitate their job search. I recommend activating your account, and following the companies in your target employer list, as well as recruiters and key contacts you have made there.

 **Meetup** (www.meetup.com) is a social networking site dedicated to making it easy for anyone to organize a local group, or find one of the thousands already **meeting face-to-face**. More than 2,000 Meetup groups get together in local communities each day. You should be able to find groups specifically tailored to your career pursuits, skills, or interests.

 Viadeo is a European professional and social network whose members include business owners, entrepreneurs, and managers. Based out of **France**, the site had 65 million members by 2014.

XING ("crossing") is a European career-oriented social networking site enabling a "small-world" networking method for professionals. Based in **Germany**, it is used by people from over 200 countries. One unique feature I like about Xing is how it displays visually how each member is connected to any other member.

The STAR Career Workbook

Weibo is the most popular social media site in China, with around 250 million registered users and over 100 million daily visitors. A hybrid of Twitter and Facebook, messages are limited to 140 characters. Users have a verified identity (this is essential if you plan to use this tool) and can brand themselves by sharing content with images, music, and video. If your target companies are headquartered in China, find a way to network on Weibo.

Promptivate provides a system for you to see all your connections, receive reminders, and most importantly, receive valuable prompts on how to engage with your important connections.

Indeed is the #1 source for job search for millions of people each month. Upload your resume and set your alerts to notify you of matching jobs that are posted. Recruiters may also contact you directly to invite you to consider their opportunities.

Glassdoor appears to capture the market for jobseekers who are researching a potential employer, by engaging the public in minimally censored reviews of companies, their management, and their practices.

EventBrite is another tool you should consider for finding events, meetings, and networking opportunities. Eventbrite is a global marketplace for live experiences, that allows people to find and create events in 190 countries. Set up your own account, or just visit the site and browse, to find interesting and relevant meetings and events in your area.

The STAR Career Workbook

Maximizing Professional Networking Sites

✦ **Complete your Profile**: Fully update your profile, including a picture, job history, overview of skills (using your Professional Introduction), and contact information.

- Use a recent, professional picture of YOU, alone. People need to be able to recognize you when you send them an invitation or a message. Use a "headshot" from your chest to the top of your head. Dress in the attire you would wear to an interview.

- For your title, tag-line, or status, use your desired job title. Do not use "Looking for a new opportunity" or a similar status. This turns away hiring managers who prefer "passive" candidates.

- Do not insert your entire resume. Give a high-level summary and a key accomplishment for each job. Go back at least 5 jobs or 10 years, whichever comes first.

- If you wish to be contacted by anyone wishing to connect with you ("open networker"), make your email address visible so that they can invite you to connect.

- Update your status every 5 to 7 days, on various days of the week, by tweaking minor points in your profile, even if repeating information. This increases your page-ranking and visibility to your network.

✦ **Build your Contacts**: Synchronize your account with your email contacts from all available sources, and then go through business cards, lists, spreadsheets, and other databases you might have, to gather more connections. Send out invitations to everyone you know, who should be online. Initially, you want to build a broad base of contacts so that you can search through your contacts to identify people who can connect you to job opportunities, or other people at your target companies.

- **Ask for and Give Recommendations:** Contact your previous co-workers, customers, managers (as appropriate), and subordinates, and ask for recommendations. Reciprocate.

- **Communicate your Search to your Contacts:** After you have built up your contacts sufficiently (100 1st level contacts, at minimum), send out messages to your contacts through the messaging or email features on the site, using your Moving Forward Statement, Professional Introduction, and Professional Objective as a template for a cover letter. Each time you add a new block of 20 or more contacts, or every 2 weeks, resend this message to all contacts.

- **Join Groups:** Join groups and actively participate. Join groups that are relevant to your career path or interests. Join at least 2 groups that will have members at higher levels of career advancement, so that you can monitor and engage with potential hiring managers.

- **Follow Companies:** Find and follow all of the companies on your target employer list.

- **Start a Group:** If you are adventurous, and you identify an interest that is not currently being served in your area, start a new group. Try not to duplicate other current efforts, and know that managing a group does take valuable time. Set it up in the easiest, lowest maintenance way. Recruit a partner or two to help you manage the group.

- **Answer Questions and Participate in Discussions:** Answering questions or participating in discussions should follow these basic rules: (1) **Relevant** to your career path; (2) **Polite**, humble, and well-written; (3) **Helpful** to the person who started the discussion or asked the question, and as helpful as possible to all potential readers.

The STAR Career Workbook

- **Start Discussions / Ask Questions:** Using the same 3 rules above, start discussions that will draw attention to your search. In some cases, you may choose to post your Moving Forward Statement, Professional Introduction, and Professional Objective as a discussion, if you are communicating with a group that appears to support that kind of communication. Often, but with caution, you will want to provide your contact information on that discussion, so that people interested in connecting with you for potential leads, can find you.

- **Post Events / Host Events:** On many social networking sites there is a feature to post events to the main calendar or to group calendars. Find external events that are particularly interesting to your career path and post information about these events to the calendar. You can notify your network and your groups of free events and paid events. Consider organizing your own group event, such as a discussion group on a topic relevant to your career path. Invite an "expert" speaker. Host it at a place where everyone can buy their own coffee, meal, or evening beverage, and you should have no cost. Consider using the Eventbrite platform, so you can capture attendee information for follow-up.

- **Search Jobs:** LinkedIn has an active job posting section. Search for jobs in your career path and apply, but don't stop there. See who you know, who might be connected to the posting organization, and make more connections at that company. You will stand out from the crowd of LinkedIn job applicants if you have a few contacts at their company. It is even more helpful if a current or former employee of that company has written a recommendation for you!

- Include newer features on LinkedIn that show off your areas of expertise, such as Blog Posts, Reading Lists, and SlideShare. The

The STAR Career Workbook

best social media and networking sites will offer advice on features you can add to improve your profile strength.

Guidance for using social media *(like Facebook):*

- Keep your content light and social, but with a professional taste.
- Limit or at least review the photos you have posted, and will be posting. Keep them tasteful; no embarrassing moments.
- Choose your Friends wisely. Remember your Friends can see information about your other Friends in your Profile.
- Stay "on message" with your Moving Forward Statement, Professional Introduction, and Professional Objective
- Stay Relevant, Polite, and Helpful. Avoid highly charged conversations, like political or protest movements. Avoid criticism directly aimed at any person, and only criticize topics or issues on which you have expertise.
- Monitor the content others put on your page, and aggressively remove anything potentially distasteful to potential employers.
- Don't get caught up in games, and off-subject chatter, as they hijack your precious time.
- Know that many employers will check you out on Facebook to try and see if there is a *"dark side"* of you. Stay on Message!
- If you are concerned about employers seeing your personal information, you can change your privacy settings so only certain people, like your friends or family, can view your profile. However, this is not helpful to your job search. Either use Facebook wisely or don't use it at all.

The STAR Career Workbook

Professional Networking and Social Media Worksheet

Site: Yes / No	Site: Yes / No	Site: Yes / No	Site: Yes / No	Quality Assurance Questions
				Upload a professional headshot photo (full color, shoulders-up, professional attire, simple background).
				Update your status with your desired job title. (Not "Seeking, Looking for… or Available").
				Enter your professional experience history (Here, you can say "open to new opportunities").
				Link your social media pages to each other, and your blog (if blogging), and/or personal website.
				Connect with 50+ family, friends, neighbors, alumni, and related personal contacts.
				Connect with 100+ professionals in your industry or field, including current & past co-workers.
				Connect with 50+ professionals at your target employers.

The STAR Career Workbook

Professional Networking and Social Media Worksheet (continued)

Site: Yes / No	Site: Yes / No	Site: Yes / No	Site: Yes / No	Quality Assurance Questions
				Find and follow the company pages of your target employers.
				Join 10+ groups relevant to your job search, your profession, and your interests.
				Send a communication about your search to at least 100 contacts.
				Engage with at least 5 of the groups you have joined through discussions or sharing content.
				Engage with 3 of the companies you are following, where possible, with comments to their updates.
				Post _daily_ status updates, comments, links to interesting articles, events, or to your own blog posts.
				Search and apply for 20 jobs, then connect with, and communicate to, a contact at each employer.

The STAR Career Workbook

Additional Ways to Use LinkedIn

(which may also apply to other SM sites)

- **Improve your Google Page Rank.** LinkedIn allows you to make your profile information available for search engines to index. Since LinkedIn profiles receive a fairly high Page Rank in Google, this is a good way to influence what people see when they search for you. To do this, create a public profile and select "Full View". Also, instead of using the default URL, customize your public profile's URL to be your actual name. To strengthen the visibility of this page in search engines, use this link in various places on the web. For example, when you comment in a blog, include a link to your profile in your signature.

- **Enhance your search engine results.** In addition to your name, you can also promote your blog or website to search engines like Google and Yahoo! Your LinkedIn profile allows you to publicize websites. There are a few pre-selected categories like "My Website", "My Company", etc. If you select "Other" you can modify the name of the link. If you're linking to your personal blog, include your name or descriptive terms in the link, and voila! Instant search engine optimization for your site. To make this work, be sure your public profile setting is set to "Full View".

- **Perform blind, reverse, and company reference checks.** Companies will typically check your references before hiring you, but have you ever thought of checking your prospective manager's references? Most interviewees don't have the audacity to ask a potential boss for references, but with LinkedIn you have a way to scope him/her out. You can also check up on the company itself, by finding the person who used to have the job that you're interviewing for. Do this by searching for job title and company, but be sure to uncheck

The STAR Career Workbook

"current titles only". By contacting people who used to hold the position, you can get the inside scoop on the job, manager and growth potential.

- **Increase the relevancy of your job search.** Use LinkedIn's advanced search to find people with educational and work experience like yours, to see where they work. For example, a programmer would use search keywords such as Ruby on Rails, C++, Python, Java, and Programmer, to find out where other programmers with these skills work.

- **Make your interview go smoother.** You can use LinkedIn to find the people that you're meeting. Knowing that you went to the same school, played the same sports, or share acquaintances is a great opportunity to establish good chemistry with your interviewer.

- **Gauge the health of a company.** Perform an advanced search for company name, and uncheck the "Current Companies Only" box. This will enable you to scrutinize the rate of turnover and whether key people are abandoning ship. Former employees usually give more candid opinions about a company's prospects, than someone who's still on board.

- **Gauge the health of an industry.** If you're thinking of investing or working in a sector, use LinkedIn to find people who worked for competitors—or even better, companies who failed.

- **Track startups.** You can see people in your network who are initiating new startups, by doing an advanced search for a range of keywords such as "stealth" or "new startup". Scan the people closest to you (1st degree connections) first.

 **The STAR Career Workbook**

Blogs and Blogging

A blog is an excellent way to establish your brand as an expert in your field. If you are a good writer, and have interesting content to share with people in your industry, or to the public in general, you should consider writing a blog.

A blog is not a place to share other people's content. You must have your own original content. If you want the blog to help your career progress, only share content related to your field and interests. This may be research, lessons you've learned, and even expanded STAR stories with guidance to readers on how they might have similar successes. Blog articles can be as short as 2 or 3 paragraphs, or as long as 3 or 4 pages, but I do not recommend making them longer than this.

Use the small worksheet on the following page to plan your blog.

- Your blog should enhance your personal brand; not someone else or another group. Make sure you can set up the blog under your own name, and that the link to your blog page can include your name.
- Remember the 3 rules of participating in discussions and questions on Social Networking sites. Your blogging should be: (1) **Relevant** to your career path; (2) **Polite**, humble, and well-written; (3) **Helpful** as possible to all potential readers.
- If you have a blog that is very opinionated on issues of politics, religion, or culture, I recommend that you do **not** reference that blog on your profiles on social networking sites, nor on your resume, or other career search documents. The only exception would be for those pursuing career fields RELEVANT to strongly opinionated content in one of these areas.
- You can host your blog on most any popular blog site, within a social networking site relevant to your field, or on general blogging sites, such as WordPress (which I use), or Blogger (which I have used); or

search BlogCatalog.com for a category you want to focus on, and either join an existing blog community or start your own.
- Make sure your blog can be found on your profile page, of any social networking sites you are using to pursue career opportunities, and keep it up to date every week or so.
- It is not important to blog every day, or even every week. More importantly, blog about issues relevant to your career path.
- When you do blog, update your social media status to reflect that you've updated your blog, preferably with a direct link back to the new article. Most blog sites will enable you to connect and share your blog posts directly to your social media pages. I am using WordPress now, specifically for this functionality, but also because of the ease of posting and tracking my posts.
- Consider if the topic you are discussing has a strong potential impact for some of your contacts, and if it does, send them a message to visit your blog.

Blog Planning Worksheet

1. What interesting and original content do you have that you could upload *now* to a blog?

2. Check out the various blog sites where you might host your blog.

Which site is most relevant or functional for your purposes?	
Will this site allow you to personally brand the blog with your name?	

The STAR Career Workbook

Open an account and set up your blog. Is it easy to use?	
Does it have the tools you need to create, edit, and share your posts?	

3. Upload your current content and get it posted and shared.

Edit the content, and then have a trusted friend or partner review it before posting it publicly.	
Insert interesting, appealing and engaging images with your content.	
Share updates and link your content to your social media pages.	
Send direct emails or communications to specific contacts alerting them to your recent blog post.	

4. What interesting and original content do you want to produce next, and when will you post it?

Content	Deadline

The STAR Career Workbook

Personal Web Pages

A personal web page is a good place to present your qualifications in a more spread out fashion. It is an interactive sales brochure of ***"product you"***. If you already have a personal website, perhaps something that came FREE with your internet or cable service, take advantage of this to build a career-focused website.

There are many different website builders available on the market, all offering a range of features, from responsive themes and hosting space, to eCommerce features. The best service really depends on what you're looking for, and whether or not the platform can meet your needs. The top website builders in 2018, according to Affiliate Marketing Corp. were Wix, GoDaddy and Web.com.

I do not recommend simply creating a one page site and sticking your resume on it. One of the pages on your site may be your resume page. However, you also need to spend some time developing more creative representations of your career experience, capabilities, and services. Utilizing some of your accomplishment stories, expand on some of your key successes. Develop a catalog of your services, centered around the individual strengths and competencies you command.

You may have the opportunity to offer your services as an independent consultant during your period of unemployment, becoming self-employed for a period of time, and you may be able to develop a sound business to carry you forward for many years. However, make sure that your personal web page incorporates your full name in the title or header, so that visitors to your site know that this is YOUR page and YOUR expertise.

The STAR Career Workbook

Personal Web Worksheet

Which site is most relevant or functional for your purposes?

Will there be a cost associated with your site? How does this fit into your budget?

Will you be able to personally brand the site with your full name? What will you call it?

What is your menu of services and planned lay-out for your site?

 *The STAR Career Workbook*

Define Your Target Market and Target Employers

Now that you have built your network and your personal brand, you need to focus on identifying your target employers. Remember, in identifying your Career Vision, you are looking for more than just a job. You are looking for an excellent match, to continue pursuing your Career Vision. Document here the variables you need to consider in selecting a target employer, then use the resources on the following pages to research and identify names of companies you should pursue.

MY CORE VALUES: (company culture where I belong)
1.
2.
3.
4.
5.

MY TOP STRENGTHS (skills transferrable to target industries)
1.
2.
3.
4.
5.
6.
7.

 **The STAR Career Workbook**

MY BEST FUNCTIONAL ROLES: (my passion and where I've had success)
1.
2.
3.
4.
5.

MY MOST APPROPRIATE TITLES:
(based on my accomplishments; not years of experience)
1.
2.
3.
4.
5.

MY MOST APPROPRIATE COMPANY SIZE FOR MY CHOICES SO FAR:
1.
2.
3.

MY GEOGRAPHIC RESTRICTIONS:
(in order of priority; moving down the list as necessary)
1.
2.
3.
4.
5.

 **The STAR Career Workbook**

Sources for Researching and Identifying Target Employers

Name	Description	URL
Inc. 500-5000	Inc. Magazine's 500 and 5000 fastest-growing companies in America.	inc.com/inc5000
Fortune magazine Rankings	Fortune ranks the world's top companies on a variety of values.	fortune.com/rankings
U.S. Department of Labor	Occupational Outlook Handbook (OOH)	bls.gov/ooh
Vault	Research and lists of companies, industries, salary info, jobs, etc.	vault.com
Glassdoor	Current and former employees anonymously review companies.	glassdoor.com
GuideStar	Research and data on non-profit organizations (with FREE quick-search).	guidestar.org
Idealist	Find non-profit people, organizations, groups, jobs, events, and more.	idealist.org
Red Herring - The Business of Technology.	Research, news, and the RedHerring lists of top technology companies.	redherring.com

The STAR Career Workbook

Target Employer Worksheets

I recommend identifying at least 3 industry types or sector to broaden your search. Use the following three worksheets to clarify each industry, and begin to identify target companies:

INDUSTRY 1	TARGET COMPANIES:	TARGET COMPANIES:
TITLES / FUNCTIONS:		
SIZE OF ORGANIZATION:		
CULTURE:		
GEOGRAPHY:		

The STAR Career Workbook

INDUSTRY 2	TARGET COMPANIES:	TARGET COMPANIES:
TITLES / FUNCTIONS:		
SIZE OF ORGANIZATION:		
CULTURE:		
GEOGRAPHY:		

The STAR Career Workbook

INDUSTRY 3	TARGET COMPANIES:	TARGET COMPANIES:
TITLES / FUNCTIONS:		
SIZE OF ORGANIZATION:		
CULTURE:		
GEOGRAPHY:		

The STAR Career Workbook

"Traditional" Job Search

Networking with your contacts, getting introduced to a hiring manager at a target company, and demonstrating your value and benefit as a solution to existing challenges they face, is the <u>historically traditional</u> means of job searching.

This is the approach I recommend.

Other than apprenticeships and journeymen opportunities, the most often hiked route to employment over the last 100 years has been through networking.

However, I understand that you will want to spend some time assessing the market for job openings, applying for those jobs, and seeing where it takes you. Why not? It's faster than ever with the internet. You can apply for 5 jobs in a day, using websites, email, and corporate career portals. So, let's talk about some ways to make that process more effective and efficient, so you can get it out of the way for the time you will need to network!

Finding Job Openings

Online Search

The web offers millions of routes to find job opportunities, so you will have to decide which you want to use early, and stick with them. Through the course of your search, you will be hit with emails and advertisements about many other internet services you can use, because the Web 2.0 Big Brothers are watching your every click, and they know you are job searching!

The STAR Career Workbook

The best and simplest Job Search tool on the web today is Indeed (www.indeed.com). Others to consider are Jobs2Careers (www.jobs2careers.com) and SimplyHired (www.simplyhired.com). Also, new to the scene is ZipRecruiter (www.ziprecruiter.com).

With these tools you can set up a **search agent**, which will email you on a daily basis, with any jobs that it finds for you on the web. Those jobs might be posted on corporate sites, job boards, government sites, or recruiting agency sites. When you follow the links they provide, you will navigate to the host page and be instructed how to apply for the position (if it is a match for you).

Leads and Associations

As **you will continue to network**, you will likely be given leads from people you have informed of your search. Some of these leads may include contact information, and often an email address of the recruiter managing the job opening. Other leads may include a link to a website where the job is posted, and other leads may just include a name of a company and the job they have open. Simply take the information you have and run a search in one of the tools mentioned, or use a raw Google search to find the link.

If you are actively involved with a local professional association, those groups will often provide leads of job openings for current members. See if there is an email distribution list for job openings and get on it. Members are usually encouraged to share leads they have found – do so. Don't be concerned with giving a lead to a "competitor". The best candidate, you, will rise to the top.

The STAR Career Workbook

Corporate Sites

You will have identified a number of **Target Employers** in your work thus far, and you will want to monitor their current job openings, as quickly as they are posted. Most large corporations have installed and integrated a robust *Applicant Tracking System* (ATS), that includes a *Career Portal* with all of their active job openings. Even small and mid-sized companies will at least have a jobs page on their website. Whenever possible, set up a complete profile on their ATS, and load your resume. Then, if their system provides the feature, set up a job agent that will email you whenever a job matches your credentials.

When you receive job notifications from your target employers, you will want to log on as quickly as possible, and complete any necessary steps to get your profile and resume submitted for the job. Don't place a strong amount of hope in this process, as many jobs posted on large corporate sites have a pre-selected candidate already in the waiting. Through your networking efforts, you want to be that pre-selected candidate!

In the case of smaller companies without a more advanced ATS, you will have to establish reminders for yourself, to return to their websites to check on their new openings. The tools mentioned above may pick up some of those for you, but they are not 100% in their effectiveness. Bookmark the career sites of your target employers, and/or keep a spreadsheet of the companies, and their career/jobs pages, so you can return regularly.

The STAR Career Workbook

Job Boards

The biggest players on the job board market are Monster (www.monster.com) and CareerBuilder (www.careerbuilder.com), but there are hundreds of job boards; some for niche skillsets, and others just new to the scene. You should **build a complete profile,** and keep an active and **updated resume** on at least 2 of these job boards. In addition, if you are a technically-focused candidate (mostly engineers), the biggest player is Dice (www.dice.com).

Craigslist (www.craigslist.com) became a player in job postings, often because it is very cheap for the job poster, and because the employer can remain anonymous if they choose to do so. Both of these features (cheap and anonymous) concern me, as they should you.

I do not advise applying to a job posting that does not reveal the name and contact information of the employer.

LinkedIn (www.linkedin.com) has a very active job posting system in play, and many recruiters are using it exclusively, to market their openings, because they can review your profile and recommendations as soon as you apply. You should take the additional time to network with whomever you can, to get additional recommendations sent in to the recruiter, from your contacts, using the tools in the LinkedIn jobs section.

There are many, many more job sites, and this chapter could not possibly cover all of those which are good, and those which are a waste of time. Ask your friends and contacts who are also job-searching, which sites they are using, get a consensus, and go with it. You don't have a lot of time to be choosey, and you don't have time to jump around among too many sites.

There are a number of new job boards that are more attuned to Social Networking/Web 2.0. Some are more locally focused, and can drive you to better networking opportunities. Check them out, ask around, and go with the sites: whether big, small, specialized, localized or homogenized, that offer you the best **ease of use, accessibility** and **results**.

Job Search Site Tracking Worksheet

Take some time now to log on to the sites you have selected to use in your search. Set up your account/user name and password, and log that information using this worksheet, or a similar version of your own. Save it in a safe place on your computer, using either MS Word or MS Excel, or similar software.

Site Name	URL	User Name	Password

 **The STAR Career Workbook**

Applying Directly to a Job Posting

Whether you are applying through a job board, corporate site, or by email directly to a recruiter, **there is just one key** to a successful application to a posted job opening. You must answer each and every item in the requirements of the posted job, and most of the items in the list of duties and responsibilities. You must clarify how your experience and accomplishments appears to be a mirror-image of their job posting. Note that this is NOT done by simply saying in a cover letter, "I am a perfect match for this job!" This may be done in a 2 column chart, a bullet-point response list, or paragraph format, with bold-facing keywords.

Before you attach and submit your resume, go through it with a fine-tooth comb, and make sure your resume backs up everything you claim in your cover letter. Note that cover letters are often skimmed over, so consider whether your resume will also do what you wanted your cover letter to do. If not, customize it, save it with a unique name, and send the customized version. Hold to the truth, but reply to their stated needs, using their language. See more help and samples in the chapter on Resumes and Cover Letters.

Tracking your Applications

The biggest reason why I don't admire the process of applying for existing job openings is the lack of control, response, and feedback you get as a candidate. If you've been on the search for a while already, or this is not your first trip to the candy store, then you know that most of your job applications seem to go off into a black hole, never to return.

The one thing you can do is to track (using a spreadsheet for example), every job you apply for, the contact (if any), the source, the website where it is posted, and the date of your application.

# The STAR Career Workbook

Then you should set up reminders to follow up, where possible, to do the following:
1. Request status on the job opening
2. Network with contacts who might influence your candidacy
3. Request recommendations
4. Request an exploratory meeting
5. Re-state your qualifications and clarify your strengths as a candidate.

In reality, you may only follow up on 25% to 50% of the many jobs you apply for, but those efforts will make you "feel" more in control of this process. And, if you work your network to get insight into the company, recommendations to the hiring manager, and so forth, after you have submitted your traditional application, your chances of getting some feedback increase exponentially.

Application Tracking Worksheet

Take some time now to create your own Application Tracking worksheet. I recommend using MS Excel or similar software. Following are sample columns you might include in your worksheet. Most headings are logical in what they should include. In the "Link to Posting" column, copy and paste the URL to the best source for the job posting, so that you can return to it at any point to reread the job description and requirements. In the Follow-up 1 through 3 fields, list the date of the follow up and a note about your results. For example, 1/28 emailed to Jean; 2/9 called to request status; 2/16 emailed and called CEO with final pitch.

- Company
- Contact Person
- Email Address
- Phone Number
- Source of Lead
- Link to Posting
- Job Title
- Apply Date
- Follow-up 1
- Follow-up 2
- Follow-up 3

The STAR Career Workbook

Communicating with HR and Corporate Recruiters

Human Resources Managers at companies where you want to work are good people. They genuinely care about people, and that is why they went into HR. These are the folks who were told from a young age, "you're good with people, and you should go into teaching or something like that." Well, they were smart enough to pursue a job that pays a little more than teaching, but now they are finding they have a very heavy workload.

In the past, there was usually about 1 HR representative for each 100 employees, but today, with automation and cost-cutting, it's more like 1:300. They may serve a population that is spread out internationally, and as diverse as turtles, cats, and dolphins.

When you communicate with an HR Manager who is screening your application, communicate your awareness of the burden on them, and seek ways to ally with them in matching you to the opportunity. Respect that they will often want to "follow the process", even if clearly, the search should be shut down, and you should be hired immediately, because no one else could be as uniquely qualified! Work with them as long as you must, to get moved forward to the next stage; hopefully that is to the hiring manager.

Corporate Recruiters today have often had some experience on both sides of the desk; with some background as a headhunter, then possibly returning to a corporate role. Others have come through the ranks at one or more similar companies, and have profound loyalty to their employer. Corporate Recruiters should be strongly networked, so you should be able to track them down on LinkedIn, Facebook and Twitter, and communicate with them outside of the applicant tracking system.

In a mature and growth-oriented company, corporate recruiters are incentivized to move the recruiting process along, and close requirements quickly, with the best talent. If you follow the advice above, on aligning your experience and accomplishments with their posted requirements, and making sure you communicate that succinctly with impact, you will win their hearts.

Corporate Recruiters Mindset:
- The philosophy is to reduce the field, to identify their top candidates quickly.
- Most work on around 15 to 25 open requisitions at a time, which is like managing 15 to 25 projects at a time, with high process (red tape).
- Looking for EXACT matches to job postings.
- Will pursue placements with least resistance.
- Will prioritize candidates internally referred.

Corporate Recruiter Strategy:
- Get a name whenever you can.
- Respond specifically to the job requirements.
- Research the company, and reference what you've learned in your cover letter.
- Let them know who you know in their organization.
- Do not discuss personal issues; avoid giving them "red flags".
- Follow up
- Follow up
- Follow up

 # The STAR Career Workbook

Working with Recruiters/Headhunters at Agencies

While there are some really good people out there, working as agency Recruiters and Headhunters, both with large agencies, specialty groups, and independents, you need to know that they do not work for you.

Follow the money.

Headhunters are paid by, and work for, the employer. No matter what the recruiters may say, ultimately, they are not on your side (at least not yours alone). Stay on your guard at all times, sharing as much as you can, to communicate your value, skills, successes, and your "message" but keep your personal business personal.

Some of the matches you find to job postings on job boards, and job searching tools, may be postings by agencies. One frustrating piece of this is when the recruiter at the agency is unwilling to give you the name of the employer, so that you can do additional research and networking. I advise you to negotiate for this information, assuring the recruiter that you will not go around them to apply for the role in another fashion, and that you will help to insure that they get credit for your referral to the job, should you be hired. If they persist in shielding this information, simply move on and focus your energy on other leads.

Quick test of a recruiter you want to continue working with:
1. A recruiter who takes time to **listen** to you.
2. A recruiter who **helps** you with your search for other jobs.
3. A recruiter who helps you with your **communication** strategy.
4. A recruiter who will **network** with you, not just for today's opportunity, but for future years to come.

 **The STAR Career Workbook**

Bottom line: work with recruiters you are comfortable with, and the ones who come strongly recommended.

How many recruiters should you engage? Just enough to cover your bases. I recommend aligning with one recruiter at a large multi-purpose agency, one recruiter at a small local-owned agency, and one recruiter at a specialty firm that focuses on a market or industry where you have target employers. Too many more alliances may infuse more chaos than you can manage into your search.

Recruiter (Agency) Mindset:
- Philosophy is to "sell" candidates to clients.
- Most work on high-volume basis, fast moving, chaotic.
- Looking for "stand-out" or "rock-star" candidates.
- Looking for most common skill sets first, then "purple squirrels".
- Will pursue placements that can close fastest.

Recruiter (Agency) Strategy:
- Look through your network for referrals of good recruiters.
- "Connect" with the recruiter; find common interests.
- Avoid sharing personal trials and "red flags".
- Give the recruiter good marketing material for you.
- Be focused on your Professional Objective, and stay on your message.
- Stay on the recruiter's radar (follow-up), but don't stalk.

The STAR Career Workbook

Getting to the Hiring Manager

Getting a face-to-face meeting with the hiring manager, other than getting a job offer, is the ultimate goal of both "traditional" job search and career networking. It is also the most difficult task when applying for an already-posted job opening. When you are an "outsider" applying for a job posting, along with 1000 other candidates, the company will typically have established multiple gates and gate-keepers, to allow the hiring manager to keep getting his daily work done, while they pre-screen and identify their top candidates.

As an outsider trying to become an insider, remember that the 4 key elements the hiring manager is looking for are:

- Compatibility – Are you qualified?
- Character – Do your professional values sync with the employer's values?
- Chemistry – Will the team "like you", and will you all be able to work well together to achieve results?
- Compensation – Do you fit with the job level and salary range they have budgeted?

3-Step Plan

I have worked with successful sales professionals to develop a 3-step plan to position your "personal brand", such that a customer will meet with you These rules apply for attracting, connecting with, and keeping the conversation rolling, with a hiring manager at a target company.
1. Be an expert in your field: Through your networking and communication efforts, establish your "personal brand" as having unique expertise in some area of your field. This can be done by offering helpful guidance to others in your field, skillfully

mentioning your key accomplishments, having excellent recommendations viewable on your web profiles, and by actively networking, both virtually and in-person, through groups that share your professional interests.

2. Work the numbers: In the chapter on Networking Basics, I introduced the concept of the "sales funnel" or pipeline. When targeting hiring managers within target companies, do not focus all of your efforts on one person with authority, but network and reach out to all persons with influence in the organization. You may establish a connection with a VP in a different department. That person may recognize your expertise and your chemistry, and recommend you to the VP you need to meet.

3. Learn and play their game: Learn the daily and weekly pattern or habits in the organization, and particularly with the hiring managers you need to reach. What days are they busy? When do they have their weekly meetings? Where do they go for lunch or happy hours? Learn which gatekeepers have influence in their daily and weekly plans. Make a plan to connect with your target hiring managers by following these habits. Learn the company lingo and speak it. Learn about their energy, hours, approach, and metrics, and adopt them.

Networking via Social Media

In my chapter on Networking through Social Media, I discuss at much greater length, the action items you will want to undertake, to network via social mediums. Use these steps to connect with as many current and former employees of your target organizations. Learn who they know, and track them to the hiring decision-makers. Meet with any people in, or formerly in the organization, who can give you valuable insights about being successful there; and especially those who can introduce and recommend you to the hiring decision-makers.

Cc: Method

The Cc: Method is used when you have 1 or 2 contacts within the organization, and you have been given the contact information for a hiring decision-maker. You will prepare an "introductory cover letter" (see the chapter on Cover Letters) in an email to the hiring manager and copy your contacts. Your first paragraph will reference your connection with these contacts, and how well you can work with them (chemistry connection), and the rest of the email will flow according to instructions. Your contacts now have a professional *nudge* to follow up with a note to the hiring manager, encouraging him/her to meet with you. Best practice is to discuss this ahead of time with each contact, and ASK them to follow up when they see your email.

Special Event Method

The Special Event Method is used when you do not have a name or contact information for the hiring manager, but you may have a general phone number, and possibly a couple of connections in the organization. You will contact whomever you can reach, hopefully one of your connections, but possibly a gatekeeper, and say that you would like to send an invitation to the hiring manager (referenced by his or her title), to a special event (happy hour for professionals in a local user group or a networking group, for example). You will ask for an email address, and if possible, a phone number (less likely to get). This method requires boldness and tact, and should be used with as much honesty as possible. In other words, there should be a 'real' special event you can invite this person to attend; an event you can easily find through your own networking efforts.

ABC / Pre-Close

In the chapter on Closing on Your Dream Job, I discuss the ABC rule: "Always Be Closing." Refer to that chapter for a review of how to pre-close throughout your efforts to get introduced to, and meet with, a hiring decision-maker.

Be Bold

It is way too easy to just email in your resume and wait for feedback, thinking you have very little power to do anything more. If you adopt this philosophy, you will continue to be lost in those black holes, with no feedback. It takes boldness and tact to continue to creatively approach an organization to get recognized, but the rewards are:

- satisfaction that you gave it your best effort,
- possibly, a more satisfying interview,
- possibly, a job.

The STAR Career Workbook

Interviewing Best Practices

Interviewing Basics
There are 3 types of interviews you will encounter:

Investigational/Informational interviews
Because you are networking, and working with your contacts, to uncover hidden opportunities, you will schedule for yourself a number of investigational or informational interviews. As you are scheduling the meeting, it may have a more casual tone, depending on who you are meeting with. It may happen onsite at the company, over coffee or lunch, or by telephone. The top preference is to schedule the meeting onsite at the target company, so that you might have an opportunity to meet other potential team members, decision-makers and hiring managers. Regardless, you will want to make sure and maintain your professionalism, and "stay on message".

TAKE TIME NOW to write down who you want to meet with in the next 3 weeks, where and when you want to meet (i.e. coffee at local coffee shop, mid-morning at his/her office), and issues you want to discuss (i.e. future openings, intro to hiring decision-makers, industry insight).

Telephone Interviews:

Generally conducted in early stages of the interviewing process, telephone interviews can often be done for the purpose of **eliminating candidates** and narrowing the field. It is especially important, therefore, that you monitor your energy, tone, and message. Stay positive, stay on message, and avoid any "red flag" issues or comments.

TAKE TIME NOW to write down the "red flag" issues that you historically bring up. (i.e. bad relationship with a former boss, gaps in employment, lack of confidence in an area, etc.), and plan now for avoiding those issues – or addressing them positively if the interviewer asks about them.

Red Flag Issue	Plan to Avoid and/or Address

Face-to-Face / Onsite Interviews:

Believe it or not, once a company has invested time in scheduling their time to bring you in, they actually **want you to succeed**. Approach these interviews, mentally, with a ***win-win attitude***. Seek to understand their needs, convey your strengths and successes, and make a match to their culture.

# The STAR Career Workbook

TAKE TIME NOW to research and document these key areas for the two most immediate companies you are pursuing for opportunities. Repeat this process for each target company. You can photo copy this page or recreate this tool in MS Excel or Word.

Company	
Top Needs	
Your key strengths/ successes	
Their company culture	

Company	
Top Needs	
Your key strengths/ successes	
Their company culture	

 # The STAR Career Workbook

Basic guidance for all interviewing situations

Tone of Voice: Remain upbeat and positive. Even over the telephone, people can hear you smile.

Energy: Keep a steady flow of energy; not hyperactive, and definitely not a zombie.

Remain indoors: ...*if on the phone.* Wind in the cell phone can ruin a good conversation and makes your interviewer wonder if you are lying out at the beach or focusing on a new job.

Remain calm ...and generally still, *if on the phone*. If you are moving around during the conversation, your breathing and movements will be heard over the phone. The interviewer will wonder if you are doing house chores, or focusing on their opportunity.

Lay out your notes: ...*if on the phone.* While the interviewer should anticipate that you might refer to your notes during a conversation, you don't want to be flipping through pages as if you are looking up answers on the fly.

Body Language: Keep your body language open and engaged, arms at your sides or on the table, leaning forward slightly.

Handshake: Firm and confident. Don't break their knuckles, but make it memorable. Don't let go too fast, but let go when they do.

Eye Contact: Keep steady eye contact, but don't scare them. When your eyes move off to recall a story, re-engage soon. Make sure you make good eye

 *The STAR Career Workbook*

	contact with everyone in the room, whether they are asking questions or not.
Attire:	The default rule for attire is business formal. This means a suit and tie for men, and a business suit or dress for women. Only when the interviewer instructs you to dress in less formal attire, should you stray from this rule. And even when you dress down, make sure you are dressed a little more formal than the standard attire of the business you are visiting.
Cologne/Perfume:	There is a saying that your odor should not enter a room before you. This applies whether you smell very good or very bad.
Hair and Hygiene:	Don't just look at yourself in the mirror. Ask someone with equal or better taste to look you over as well. Remain generally conservative with hairstyle, nails, etc. If you have yattoos and piercings other than earrings, it is best to keep them covered or removed until you know more about the company.
Accessories:	You might think that they won't notice your shoes. Your feet will be under a table most of the time, right? No, they will notice. Have them match your outfit, lean to the dressier side, and have them clean, polished, and scuff-free.

Men: wear dark and new dress socks (i.e. if wearing navy blue pants, wear navy or black socks with cordovan or black shoes). Yes, they

The STAR Career Workbook

will notice. Also, men: wear a belt; and your belt should match your shoes.

Women: Avoid excessive jewelry, dangling chains and bracelets that might clink and clank on the table.

What to bring: In a nice, professional portfolio notebook, bring 1 copy of your resume and 2 business/calling cards for each person you are scheduled to meet. Bring a file folder with printed research material you've gathered about the company. Sketched out on your notepad, have the top questions you want answered about the company, team, and opportunity. Down the left hand margin of the top page, write the keywords that will remind you of your top 5 STAR stories that you want to convey and use, in response to various interview questions.

The 5 C's

In every interview, there are 5 basic areas where you must make a match, to be moved forward or offered a job. Throughout the interview, you must remain cognizant of how well you have addressed each of these areas:

1. Competency: Have you sufficiently demonstrated that you have all of the required (and preferred) knowledge, skills, and abilities? If you are not sure, ask! Within the context of discussing your STAR accomplishments, be cognizant of how you are communicating your skills-match. If there is a formal job description, make sure you have it in hand, and that you are getting each requirement checked off that list.

2. **Chemistry:** Often considered to be the most important consideration, chemistry with the people in the organization can make or break you. Do you relate well with your potential new co-workers? Search for common interests and values. Allow some of the conversations to drift into these areas before attempting to bring things back to the job at hand. Allow yourself to smile and laugh when appropriate, and monitor when your interviewers are showing that they enjoy your company.

3. **Character:** Do your values match the values of the organization? You will have researched the company's stated values, and during your interview you will ask more detailed questions about what you've seen. As you confirm and refine your understanding of the company's values, you must also adequately communicate how your values make a match.

4. **Culture:** Each organization builds a unique culture, made up of the various traditions within the organization. Is it a very energetic organization focused on branding and product identification? Do they stay late, and burn the candle at both ends, or is it a more balanced commitment? Are they environmentally conscious? Do they value community service? Does your new team have some regular lunch or happy hour traditions? During the course of your interview, you'll have to identify that you fit well with these traditions.

5. **Compensation:** Does their target compensation range intersect with yours? Later, in the discussions on negotiating offers, I will cover how to determine your target salary range, and how to acquire the employer's target salary range. It is important to insure that you are a fit within their budget, and likewise, that their target salary range is acceptable to you. Don't be afraid of the compensation conversation!

The STAR Career Workbook

The Salary Question

The salary question will often come up in early rounds of screening and interviewing. The purpose of an interviewer asking this question *early* is, to see if you should be *eliminated* from consideration due to too high (and in some remote cases – too low) expectations. In this case, you want to follow these priorities:

1. Avoid: First respond with a question about whether the topic of compensation can wait, until everyone is 100% sure you are a match to their needs. It is always in your best interest to delay this conversation until they can fall more in love with you.

2. Evade: If they want to discuss it now, give a general answer that you are seeking a market-based salary commensurate with the role and your education, skills, and experience.

3. Ask: If pressed for a number, ask the interviewer if they have a range in mind for the position you would assume. If their range overlaps with yours, respond with acceptance. If their range is close, but not quite at your level, respond that it "sounds pretty close" to what you had in mind, and that you are confident that you will get to a win-win number.

4. Give Range: If they don't have a range in mind, and they indicate that they must have a salary figure from you to move forward, give a range.

    Before you develop your own range, which should be based on your current financial lifestyle, budget, and career progression, you should also research the **MARKET** salary ranges for your target jobs, positions, and roles. I recommend using multiple online sites to develop sound research behind your decision, such as PayScale.com, Indeed.com/Salary, and the U.S.

The STAR Career Workbook

Department of Labor (DOL.gov). I also recommend researching "from the street" with people you know. Ask people who are a few weeks ahead of you in their job search. Find out what offers they are seeing from potential employers. Check out these sources and pull in some numbers to this worksheet. This should give you a fair average salary which you should be expecting.

Source	Min	Mid	Max
Payscale.com			
Indeed.com/Salary			
Another site:			
Another site:			
Word from the street			
Word from the street			
Average			

Now that you have a fair assessment of the MARKET range, it's time for you to decide on your true and most comfortable range. This may be higher than your researched market averages, based on your particular successes, your budget needs, your unique combination of education or experience, or the more influential organizations where you've worked.

It may also be lower, based on your desire to make a transition, or willingness to take a step back to gain security, peace, or geographic stability. Think about these factors now, before locking in on your acceptable range.

Regardless of your direction, for negotiating purposes, I recommend stating a range that begins with your lowest acceptable salary plus a 10% negotiating buffer and spanning *about* $10,000. Example:

Your true lowest acceptable salary:	$80,000
Your 10% negotiating buffer:	+$8,000
What you tell them is your lowest acceptable salary:	$88,000
What you tell them is the top-end of your salary range:	$100,000

TAKE TIME NOW to think through your acceptable salary range, so you are prepared for these questions.

Your true lowest acceptable salary:	$
Your 10% negotiating buffer:	+$
What you tell them is your lowest acceptable salary:	$
What you tell them is the top-end of your salary range:	$

The STAR Career Workbook

Assessments of your Technical Skills and Knowledge

It is fair to expect that a potential employer may test you on your technical skills and knowledge. Be aware that:
- Anything required in the job description may be tested.
- Anything you claim to know may be tested.
- Anything you have put on your resume can be tested.

Employers may use written tests.
- Sent to you in advance, and returned before a phone or onsite interview. In this case, make sure you prepare. Take all of the time you are allowed to thoroughly complete the exercise, and return it just before the deadline.
- Given via an online testing platform.
    o You may have a limited time to prepare. If you were not warned before the meeting, that an online test would be given, it is acceptable to postpone until you can prepare.
    o You may have limited time to answer each question. Take all of the time you are given, and do not rush your answers.
    o You may be tracked on whether you stay on the testing site, or toggle to another window for answers; whether you are warned about this or not. If you have been warned, then you should be prepared, and you should NOT "game" the test by searching online for answers. Stick with what you know and do your best.
- Given in person to every candidate brought in for an onsite interview.
    o If you were not warned before the meeting that this would be asked of you, it is acceptable to ask for a re-scheduling, but this may be considerably awkward, and it is often best to proceed to take the test. Stick with what you know and do your best.
    o The knowledge or skills should be clearly identified by the job description to which you applied; and you should be

able to answer them quickly and accurately; or you are not interviewing for the right job!

Employers may use white boarding exercises during the interview.

- As with onsite written tests, your discussion during an onsite interview, should be wrapped around the skills or experiences previously identified in the job description.
- If you are prompted to illustrate an example on the whiteboard, no matter how subtle the queue may appear, stand up, grab the marker, and be bold with your presentation.
- The interviewer may only hint that you could diagram your answer on the board; take charge and do it!
- Your answers should flow from skills or experiences in your own resume. Make sure you reference these examples during your presentation.

Employers may invite you to prepare a presentation, to give in front of a group of decision makers.

- Prioritize this assignment. Suspend all other job searching efforts until you perfect your presentation.
- Do not dust off an old presentation; conduct new research.
- Include something personal about you; remember the 5 C's.
- Include something very recent and related to the employer, and especially the industry.
- Have a good friend or family member review your presentation for typo's, grammatical errors, etc.
- Practice! Check your timing to make sure you do not go over.
- Rehearse your presentation in front of an audience or friends who are in the industry. You want to rehearse in front of people who can critique your content.

 **The STAR Career Workbook**

Behavioral Interviews vs. Traditional Interviews

Traditional job interviews usually consist of a review of your resume followed by some stock questions like:
- What type of Manager do you work best with?
- What are your top 3 strengths and your top 3 weaknesses?
- Why do you think you are the best candidate for this job?

Then the interviewer may ask what he or she considers "Situational Questions".
- How would you address an upset customer?
- If you saw someone stealing from the company, what would you do?
- If your laptop went dark and was non-responsive, what are the steps you'd take?

Behavioral-based interviewing gets a more objective set of facts to make employment decisions. The process of behavioral interviewing is much more probing than "traditional" interviewing.

The premise behind **behavioral interviewing** is that the most accurate predictor of future success is past success in similar situations. Behavioral interviewing, in fact, is said to be 55 percent predictive of future on-the-job behavior, while traditional interviewing is only 10 percent predictive.

In a **traditional job interview**, you can usually get away with telling the interviewer what he or she wants to hear. When you are asked situational questions that start out "How would you handle this situation?", you have minimal accountability. How does the interviewer know if you would really react the way you say you would?

In a behavioral interview, however, it's much more difficult to give responses that are untrue to your character. When you start to tell a behavioral story, the behavioral interviewer will pick it apart to try to get at the specific behavior(s) they want to assess. The interviewer will probe further for more detail, asking questions such as, "What were you thinking at that point?" or "Tell me more about your meeting with that person". If you've told a story that's anything but totally honest, your response will not hold up through probing questions.

Employers use the behavioral interview technique to evaluate a candidate's experiences and behaviors, so they can determine the applicant's potential for success. The interviewer identifies job-related experiences, behaviors, knowledge, skills, and abilities that the company has decided are desirable in a particular position.

The employer then structures very pointed questions to elicit detailed responses aimed at determining if the candidate possesses the desired characteristics. Questions (often not even framed as a question) typically start out with: "Tell about a time..." or "Describe a situation..." Many employers use a rating system to evaluate selected criteria <u>during the interview</u>.

As a candidate, you must be equipped to answer behavioral interview questions thoroughly. Obviously, you can prepare better for this type of interview if you know which skills the employer has determined are necessary for the job you seek. Researching the company, and talking to people who work there, will enable you to focus on the kinds of behaviors the company wants. Reviewing the job description or job posting (if you have one) is also an obvious source, to understand what behaviors they deem important.

The STAR Career Workbook

In the interview, your response needs to be specific and detailed. Candidates who tell the interviewer about particular situations, which relate to each question, will be far more effective and successful than those who respond in general terms.

Reference: **A Foot in the Door: Networking Your Way into the Hidden Job Market** (Katharine Hansen, Ph.D.; published by Ten Speed Press)

One of the keys to success in interviewing is practice, so I encourage you to take the time to work out answers to these questions using the **STAR method**. Be sure not to memorize your answers. The key to interviewing success is, simply being prepared for questions, and having a mental outline to follow in responding to each question. The **STAR method** gives you that outline. Other versions of the STAR method will NOT have my secret ingredient: *Trials.*

Review that method again here:

- **S**ituation: describe the job you were in and your responsibility.
- **T**rial: describe a barrier or difficulty you faced; or the problem you needed to solve.
- **A**ctions: describe the action you took to address the trial.
- **R**esults: describe the results you achieved, which helped the company's bottom line, using *Hard Numbers*: i.e. dollars, percentages, time, headcount, etc.

 *The STAR Career Workbook*

PREPARE

- Identify 6-8 key STAR stories where you demonstrated top behaviors and skills that this employer should be seeking, based on your review of the job description, and your pre-interview networking.
- Vary your examples; don't take them all from just one past job.
- Use recent examples.

STAR story 1

STAR story 2

STAR story 3

STAR story 4

STAR story 5

STAR story 6

STAR story 7

STAR story 8

 *The STAR Career Workbook*

Sample behavioral-based interview questions:

- Describe a situation in which you were able to use persuasion to successfully convince someone to see things your way.

- Describe a time when you were faced with a stressful situation that demonstrated your coping skills.

- Give me a specific example of a time when you used good judgment and logic in solving a problem.

- Give me an example of a time when you set a goal and were able to meet or achieve it.

- Tell me about a time when you had to use your presentation skills to influence someone's opinion.

- Give me a specific example of a time when you had to conform to a policy with which you did not agree.

- Please discuss an important written document you were required to complete.

- Tell me about a time when you had to go above and beyond the call of duty in order to get a job done.

- Tell me about a time when you had too many things to do and you were required to prioritize your tasks.

- Give me an example of a time when you had to make a split second decision.

- Tell me about a time you were able to successfully deal with another person even when that individual may not have personally liked you (or vice versa).

- Tell me about a difficult decision you've made in the last year.

- Give me an example of when you showed initiative and took the lead.

- Tell me about a recent situation in which you had to deal with a very upset customer or co-worker.

- Give me an example of a time when you motivated others.

- Tell me about a time when you delegated a project effectively.

- Give me an example of a time when you used your fact-finding skills to solve a problem.

- Describe a time when you anticipated potential problems and developed preventive measures.

- Tell me about a time when you were forced to make an unpopular decision.

- Please tell me about a time you had to fire a friend.

TAKE TIME NOW… The following pages outline more samples of behavioral based questions. Next to each sample question, make a note of which STAR story you would use to answer that question, and any special pieces to that story you need to bring out to address the interviewer's specific concerns.

 *The STAR Career Workbook*

Sample Question	Your STAR Story
• Describe a situation in which you were able to use persuasion to successfully convince someone to see things your way.	
• Describe a time when you were faced with a stressful situation that demonstrated your coping skills.	
• Give me a specific example of a time when you used good judgment and logic in solving a problem.	
• Give me an example of a time when you set a goal and were able to meet or achieve it.	
• Tell me about a time when you had to use your presentation skills to influence someone's opinion.	
• Give me a specific example of a time when you had to conform to a policy with which you did not agree.	
• Please discuss an important written document you were required to complete.	
• Tell me about a time when you had to go above and beyond the call of duty in order to get a job done.	

The STAR Career Workbook

Sample Question	Your STAR Story
• Tell me about a time when you had too many things to do, and you were required to prioritize your tasks.	
• Give me an example of a time when you had to make a split second decision.	
• What is your typical way of dealing with conflict? Give me an example.	
• Tell me about a time you were able to successfully deal with another person, even when that individual may not have personally liked you (or vice versa).	
• Tell me about a difficult decision you've made in the last year.	
• Give me an example of a time when you tried to accomplish something, and failed.	
• Give me an example of when you showed initiative and took the lead.	
• Tell me about a recent situation in which you had to deal with a very upset customer or co-worker.	

 ## The STAR Career Workbook

Sample Question	Your STAR Story
• Give me an example of a time when you motivated others.	
• Tell me about a time when you delegated a project effectively.	
• Give me an example of a time when you used your fact-finding skills to solve a problem.	
• Tell me about a time when you missed an obvious solution to a problem.	
• Describe a time when you anticipated potential problems and developed preventive measures.	
• Tell me about a time when you were forced to make an unpopular decision.	
• Please tell me about a time you had to fire a friend.	
• Describe a time when you set your sights too high (or too low).	

 **The STAR Career Workbook**

Questions – You Must Ask Questions – At Interviews

Following virtually every interview you'll be asked, "What questions do you have for me?" Do you know what to ask? Do you know what not to ask? This is a critical time of the interview where you must perform. You have the opportunity to show you've thought about the job and what is important to you. Asking good questions can set you apart from other applicants. Asking bad questions can drop you from consideration. My suggestion is to have several written down and ready to ask, prior to your interview. Even if the interviewer has already covered your questions, you can still go through your list to show you were prepared. Mention to them what your questions were. Have the interviewer elaborate on a couple of them.

A few good questions to ask:

- What do you like about working here?
- What do successful people in your organization have in common?
- If I am successful, what are the opportunities for advancement, and/or additional responsibility?
- What is the company culture like?
- What values does the organization hold most important?
- Why do customers do business with you, instead of your competitors?
- Where do you see the business five years from now?
- Is there anything you'd change about the company?

The STAR Career Workbook

When in doubt, there are 4 solid questions you can ask of each interviewer:

1. How did you progress into this position you hold now?
   (gets your interviewer comfortable; people enjoy telling their story)
2. Where do you see this company going over the next 10-20 years?
   (shows that you are interested in longevity with the company)
3. What is the chemistry like on the team with which I will be working?
   (shows that you are interested in connecting within the organization)
4. In my first (10, 30, 90) days on this job, what are the most pressing challenges I need to address?
   (puts you, visually, in the chair of the job, and shows you are ready to deliver results)

Follow up and Thank you Letters after Interviews

After each interview, regardless of the type, you must follow up, and you must get thank you letters to everyone you met. You will need to get a business card or the contact information for everyone you meet, so that you can send each one of them a personalized and customized thank you letter.

- Thank you letters should be sent within one day of your interview. Sooner the better.
- Thank you letters **can** be sent by email.

Thank you letters must acknowledge the valuable time of the interviewer, and are most effective if you identify something you can praise your interviewer for. Did this interviewer provide you with very good insights into the needs of the company, outline the organizational structure for you, or just ask you really good and tough questions? Compliment them for these behaviors.

Thank you letters are also your opportunity to re-emphasize your Professional Introduction or Positioning Statement, and relate the core strengths you bring to the opportunity. Tie these facts back into what you learned during your interview, about the most pressing needs of the organization.

Follow up!

It is up to you to follow up after your interviews. Your recruiter is managing 19 other open requisitions, and hundreds of other candidate relationships. The hiring manager and his team are getting back to their "day jobs". Timing is critical. You want to appear highly motivated, and I do not advocate being shy at this time.

- If your interviewer agrees to contact you within 3 business days with feedback, call him on day 4.
- If you indicate that you will touch base in "about a week", to check status, call in 3 days.

The goal of your follow up is to keep the process moving. Ask for the next meeting, ask for the next introduction. Ask for status on your candidacy.

You can also begin to practice pre-closing and closing techniques during these engagements. See the section that follows, on CLOSING, for more guidance.

 *The STAR Career Workbook*

Closing on Your Dream Job

In sales, we follow the ABC rule: "Always be closing". The same is true for interviewing. Every interview, even investigational/informational interviews and pre-screening calls, have target results. In an informational interview, your goal is to get introduced to a decision-maker within the organization, to uncover a hidden job opportunity, or to position yourself as their next target hire. In a pre-screening call, your goal is to be advanced to a face-to-face interview, and placed high on the interest list.

You will achieve none of these goals without asking for them.
- "Who can you introduce me to today, to determine if I have value for your company?"
- "What is the greatest challenge you face right now, that I can help resolve?"
- "When you are ready to bring on your next new team member, how would you rate my position for that seat? What do I need to do to be #1?"
- "What are the next steps we need to take in the interview process? Can we check the calendar now to get that scheduled?"

Pre-Closing
Pre-closing is a technique that gets the person you are speaking with to visualize you in the job, on their team, or working in their company. Using special language in your questions, answers, and comments, you insert yourself into their line of sight. Here are some examples:
- "In my first 30 days on this job, what are the most pressing challenges I need to address?"
- "What can you tell me about the team I will be working with? What is their chemistry?"

- "I really like what I am hearing about your company. It is very consistent with my goals, and with my past accomplishments. I can't wait to get started!"
- "I have really connected with you and your team, and have identified a great match between your goals and challenges and my own goals and accomplishments. Would you agree?"

Choice between 2 Positives

The "choice between two positives" technique is a pre-closing technique that really helps your target help you. You make an **assumptive close** on the goal; whether that is a next meeting or a job offer.

- "I am available to come in for a face-to-face meeting on Tuesday in the afternoon, or Thursday in the morning. Which is better for you?"
- "I can start as soon as February 4, or would February 11 be better for you?"

Asking for the Job

You likely won't get the job if you don't ask for it. But the question needs to be delivered with tact. Here are some examples:

- "I believe this interview has been outstanding, and I am ready to join your team. Can we look at the calendar and set a start date?"
- "I can start as soon as March 4. How does that sound?"

The STAR Career Workbook

Negotiating Your Offer

Effective Negotiating Begins with Knowledge

Prior to starting your search, or at least before you wrap up your interviews, you will need to conduct sufficient research to understand the dynamics of the position you are hunting. You will need to research the appropriate salary ranges, benefits, perks, and working environment, of the positions you are targeting. This knowledge arms you for the negotiating table.

Understand your potential role, duties, deliverables and accountabilities.

Investigate the job description and ask significant questions throughout your interview, about your potential role, title, duties, and accountabilities. In the negotiating phase, cover those items again. This reminds everyone in the discussion of the VALUE you will have in their organization.

Understand how your qualifications, experiences, and past successes match the companies' stated requirements.

During the interview process, observe connections between your past successes, and your qualifications to the job description, and to the questions asked and answered. Seek acknowledgement during the interview that you've demonstrated that match. It is best to frame this as a question. "Did that example demonstrate success in the area you asked about?" "Do my qualifications appear to be a match with your requirements?"

During negotiations, you can bring up the various times, during previous discussions, that you demonstrated a clear match. In any cases where you clearly EXCEEDED their expectations, remind them again during negotiations.

Understand the Company's Pain

Prior to interviewing, your research should include many sources of information, including online research on the company's website, financial sites, and news sites. You also will want to talk to as many past and current employees as possible, to get a handle on the current market situation, and their pain points. During interviews, you will want to tactfully explore all challenges you might face in your position, and especially the challenges the company faces, which you are confident you can address. During negotiations, you can remind the hiring manager of the VALUE you will bring to the organization, in your ability to address these pains. As appropriate, you can describe the potential savings, profit, or efficiencies you will help them build.

Understand the Market Salary Range

I've already had you think through an appropriate salary range, based on market conditions, and based on your lifestyle, budget, and career progress. You will want to adjust that range, based on each of the above variables. **This is why it is essential to avoid stating your absolute salary range until after the interviewing is complete!**

The Salary Question, Part 2

After you have had successful interviews and meetings, and the decision maker is ready to talk about your future with the organization, the salary question will come up, possibly again, if it was worked out before. Generally, I recommend the exact same 4 step approach. It is simply always best for the company to state their numbers first.

At this stage, however, if the decision maker is asking you what you need in the way of salary, you also have the leverage to ask, "Does this mean you are ready to make me an offer?" If the answer is yes, and you can get them to at least give you a range, it is safest to target a number in their range that sounds fair to you. Shoot as high in their range, as you feel comfortable doing. Use intentional language in your delivery, such as...

"Based on what I am hearing from you, with regard to your range and the value I bring to the organization, I believe that $XXX,000 is a fair target. What do you think?"

If in fact, the stated salary, or range they intend to offer, is well below what you believe to be fair, don't panic, and don't bail out. Use the following negotiating tactics:

First, stay silent for a few seconds. They need to know that something is a little wrong, and silence communicates this best. If you are face to face with the offering individual, you can also give body language, which shows your concern. This might be a frown or slight scowl, but don't be aggressive with this look. You can also lean back in your chair, rub your chin, or scratch your head. But do not fold your arms. Folding your arms indicates a defensive posture, not a willingness to negotiate.

Then, ask a question. The question you will ask is, "Can you tell me more about the package that may come with that salary offer?" You may find that the company offers an amazing bonus structure, or an awesome benefits plan, that is worth the deficiency in salary. In that case, it's time to CLOSE THE DEAL. Say "yes", ask for the written offer letter, and start talking about your start date.

What if the "package" is not that great?

It is not a sin to negotiate! If your upbringing or culture is not one that cultivates negotiating, now is the time to learn these skills. The simplest way to engage, is to keep asking questions about what might be available to supplement their offer. Be precise about the elements of their offer that appear to be low, and just ask politely what they can do to improve those elements.

When you believe that they have exhausted their available offer range and other perks, and you still are not at a fair offer for the value you bring to the table, let them know. Use tact.

Take them back through the interview. Remind them again of the areas where you exceeded their expectations. Review how you will create value, by repeating your past successes in their company. Review how you stand apart as their top candidate. Remind them that they selected you as their top candidate, and that it would appear that they want to get you onboard. Then...

Ask for the specific number you need, on each element of their offer, or the one element that has remained uncomfortable. And after naming these numbers, stay silent. You will be tempted to say things like, you are flexible, or that you might accept their current offer. Say nothing at this moment. This protects you from these temptations.

Sample Script to Ask for a Better Offer:

"I am so glad we've made it to this point, where you are ready to make me an offer, because I believe I can bring a great deal of value to this organization. In our interview time, I was able to share with you how I was able to help my previous employer by.......... and I am ready to repeat that success for you. I firmly believe that a fair base salary offer

The STAR Career Workbook

for that value is going to be around $XXX,000. What can you do to get me closer to that number? "

After all of this negotiating, you still may not get everything you asked for. If the job is great, the company is great, the team is great, the manager is great, and the offer is an improvement on your current circumstances, then you should accept it. God may have a purpose in mind for you at this company, and sacrificing some of your expectations on compensation may be His will for you. In His Word, God says,

- "For I know the plans I have for you, declares the Lord, plans to prosper you and give you hope and a future." Jeremiah 29:11

- "Forget the former things; do not dwell on the past. See, I am doing a new thing! Now it springs up; do you not perceive it? I am making a way in the wilderness and streams in the wasteland." Isaiah 43:16, 18-19 NIV

- "You crown the year with your bounty, and your carts overflow with abundance." Psalm 65:11

As a review, these are the steps for the salary negotiation:
1. Restate and clarify the current offer.
2. Ask what else is included in the offer, such as bonus, equity, vacation, benefits, etc.
3. Review the interview.
4. Review how you will create value by repeating your past successes.
5. Review how you stand apart as their top candidate.
6. Ask for more salary, bonus or benefits, as needed.
7. Get the offer in writing.
8. Agree on acceptance date.

 **The STAR Career Workbook**

An offer is only an offer when it is put in writing

No matter how well you know the decision maker, how great you feel about the opportunity, or how giddy you are about getting to this point in your arduous job search journey, you must get an offer in writing.

Likewise, nothing you say about wanting the job, a potential start date, or your 30-60-90 day plans, constitute a commitment on your part until you receive, review, and accept their written offer, with a written acceptance.

Don't make any plans. Don't frame your kids' newest pictures for your new desk. Don't start packing your favorite books to take into the office. And if you are still employed somewhere, DON'T QUIT until you have received, reviewed, and accepted their written offer with a written acceptance.

Before you quit your current job or job search…

There are other considerations you should make for when you quit your current job, if you are still employed; or when you might stop your search and interviews for other opportunities.

1. Is their offer contingent on you successfully completing an extensive background and reference check?
    - If their background check covers simple things that you know you will pass, then you are safe.
    - Otherwise, you should consider waiting for a positive outcome.

2. Is their offer contingent on you acquiring a license, clearance or other government certification? You should wait until it is clear this will be obtained for you.

 *The STAR Career Workbook*

3. Do you need a visa or other work authorization in the United States or other country where you intend to work? Wait for the attorneys involved to clear you for work before making your move.

You may also have other considerations about your current employer or personal situation, which you should work out, before planning and executing your move.

1. Do you have a critical milestone with a current project, which on completion, would give your career a significant boost? It may be best to negotiate a start date with your new employer to allow you time to complete this milestone. However, do not put your new job in jeopardy.

2. Are you working on a side project or consulting gig during a period of unemployment? How much time do you need to wrap things up enough to give your new employer your full attention?

3. What are your legal obligations on the number of days you must give notice to your current employer? You might choose to wait until you are at the last day for that notice period, before announcing your departure.

4. Do you have unused vacation, that you cannot claim for cash, on your termination? How can you use that well-deserved time off before you leave for another new employer?

5. Is there an upcoming bonus pay out or vesting of stock? Can you postpone your announcement, or at least your last day of employment so that you can collect that earned income?

The STAR Career Workbook

Alternative Career Moves

This chapter will provide an "idea list" of alternative career moves, and a brief conversation about each. If you are interested in pursuing any of these paths, more research will be required. There is simply no way to go as in-depth here as I would like, or as you would require. You will want to also do some of your own investigation, using your favorite search engine, and your most reliable mentors and network contacts.

Consulting, Contracting, and Temporary Gigs

The workload for independent contractors is on the rise, as companies continue looking for ways to cut costs, while maintaining productivity levels. In recent years, you might see around 5 contractors for every 100 employees. That may not seem significant, but you can expect to see those numbers maintain, and even increase, as the economy continues to tighten the purse strings on employers.

A contracting or temporary gig can be a good alternative if you have been on the job hunt for a few months, need to build some experience, and need to bring in some income. It is also a good way to ease back into the workforce if you have been out of your field for some time, attending to a personal commitment.

If you're a recent grad, between jobs, thinking about changing careers, independent or adventurous, then contracting or temping might be right for you.

Focus on obtaining gigs that allow you to demonstrate your expertise, while advancing your skills.

Consulting as a Career

Building a career out of consulting or contracting is tough, but rewarding. You've got to know going in to the effort that each engagement is temporary, but the long-term experience you are building is permanent. Initially, you may need to contract through other firms that have been in the business for many years, but eventually you may wish to evolve your efforts into a business entity of your own. I recommend that if you are even thinking of developing a career out of consulting or contracting, that you take the initial steps to set up a business: incorporating, setting up a financial structure, and documenting your business plans.

Consulting as a new Business

Evolving from individual consultant to consulting practice takes planning, commitment, and usually, some partners. Most importantly, you've got to develop your own customers. I believe that you will not be successful, in the fullest sense, until you are no longer 2nd or 3rd on the totem pole, but when you own the direct customer relationship. The first true test, then, of whether you are ready to transition from contractor to consulting business owner, is enough paying customers (of your own) to cover your salary(ies), taxes, and expenses.

 # The STAR Career Workbook

Building a new Business from the Ground Up

If you have been building a product, designing a new system, or developing a patent, maybe now is the time to move that effort forward, into a new business. Building a business from the ground up will take considerable resources, both financial and otherwise. Some efforts can be built from one's home or garage. However, others may take loans, investors and partners. Be prepared, in any case, to let go of some of the control on your business. If it is going to fly, it has to flap its own wings!

Tips for Successful Business Planning

Conduct a full SWOT Analysis. Assess your strengths, weaknesses, opportunities, and threats. What is your biggest advantage over the competition? What do they have over you? How much risk do you need to face? Establish your best plan of attack, considering both potential, and risk.

Analyze your current situation. Ask yourself if there are better ways to be doing things. The important thing is to streamline and maximize your efforts, so that you are spending less time, effort, and money than you're getting a return on. Are there processes you can make more efficient? Establish your priorities based on how you can improve on what you've already put in place.

Develop a plan. Sit down and physically write out your plan. You didn't go into your business startup with just a bunch of ideas floating around in your head, and you can't survive that way either. Establish goals, a timeline, a budget, and a plan of attack.

Take Action! Once you've developed a plan that you feel will work for your business, put it in action. The best laid plans mean nothing if you don't take the time to schedule your efforts and follow your plan. Of

The STAR Career Workbook

course, you'll find times when you need to be flexible, and things don't always work out the way you planned, but if you have an overall goal in mind, and you have designed a process for it, you should do your best to stick to it.

Maintain. Don't let the wind go out of your sails, regardless of how successful you've been with your plan. Just because you've exceeded expectations, doesn't mean you should abandon your plan; if it works, keep at it! On the other hand, if you're facing obstacles or failures, don't give up hope. The plan may need a little reworking once the realities of business have worked their way through your estimated results, but even a plan that needs review is better than no plan at all. Periodically evaluate how things are going and adjust the plan accordingly.

Buying an Existing Business

Shop your area for successful small businesses that you might buy. Search over 48,000 businesses for sale by category and/or state at www.BizBuySell.com. Over 42,000 businesses are for sale on one of the Internet's largest business for sale exchanges at www.BizQuest.com.

When you buy an existing business, you are also buying their customers, their equipment and inventory, and their debts. Check them out thoroughly, ideally with the help of a consultant, agent, or attorney.

Obviously, this will take financial resources. Funding, and where to get it, is a major topic among business owners. One of the strongest sources is an SBA (Small Business Administration) loan. More information can be found at www.SBA.gov. There are four loan programs within the SBA, but most American banks or lenders (called Participants in the SBA) provide loans through the basic 7(a) loan program. There is not an official SBA loan application, but rather you pick a lender you feel comfortable with, and submit a commercial loan application through them. Tell them about your interest in SBA backing. The lender then

decides if they need the SBA to guarantee the loan, or if they'll make the loan in house. Check out: www.sba.gov/loans-grants.

Buying in to a Franchise

If you want to get into business for yourself, but are unsure which venture is best for you, franchises offer a ton of options. The great thing about franchising is that while you're operating your own business, you're not on your own. Franchises offer support for all types of different operating concerns, including choosing and equipping a location, branding, establishing best processes, and maintaining a quality business. While some small business owners might find the franchising process a bit stifling (because there are some areas where control is limited), for many, a franchise can turn into an easy success.

Sources for Entrepreneurial Adventures

U.S. Small Business Administration: www.sba.gov
- Programs and services to help you start, grow, and succeed with a new small business.

The National Home-Based Business Association: www.tnhbba.com
- Membership fee required. Small Business and Home-Based business advice, ideas, and resources.

Bplans: www.bplans.com
- FREE: 500+ Sample Business Plans, as well as guidance and resources.

AllBusiness.com: www.allbusiness.com
- A D&B company, provides many topics on starting a business, buying a franchise, getting sales, and more.

The STAR Career Workbook

Multi-Level Marketing

If you have a strong sales personality, and you love selling your concepts and ideas to other people, you might consider a multi-level marketing opportunity. Chances are you won't have to look too far. These opportunities have a way of finding you first!

Multi-level marketing (MLM), is a form of **Network Marketing** (however the terms are often used interchangeably). It is a marketing strategy that compensates promoters of direct selling companies, not only for product sales they personally generate, but also for the sales  of others they introduced to the company. The products and company are usually marketed directly to consumers and potential business partners, by means of relationship referrals and word of mouth marketing. Independent, unsalaried salespeople of multi-level marketing, referred to as distributors (or associates, independent business owners, dealers, franchise owners, sales consultants, consultants, independent agents, etc.), represent the parent company, and are awarded a commission, based upon the volume of product sold through each of their independent businesses (organizations). Independent distributors develop their organizations by either building an active customer base, who buy direct from the parent company, or by recruiting a *downline* of independent distributors who also build a customer base, thereby expanding the overall organization. Additionally, distributors can also earn a profit by retailing products they purchased from the parent company at the wholesale price.

Great caution should be used in evaluating and deciding on a MLM opportunity. Do not let friendships, emotions, amazing pitches, or desperation, be the momentum. Keep a level head. In fact, let your gut keep you in check. If you get a sick feeling when you are listening to the pitch, or reading over the option, it's probably for a good reason. The biggest question you must answer is whether you are looking at a legitimate opportunity, or a Pyramid Scheme.

# The STAR Career Workbook

A Pyramid Scheme is a MLM which focuses more on recruiting other investors to the program, than on selling a legitimate product with a strong available market. You can recognize these opportunities when the conversation is more about the riches you can earn by recruiting all of your friends and family to the program, than it is about selling a great product with a great brand.

On the other hand, MLMs **are** for some people, and **some** people have had good success with them.

Work from Home Options

For many good reasons, you may be considering the option of creating a work-from-home job, business, or career. You may be a single parent or taking care of an aging parent. While work-from-home-options do save considerable resources in commute time, office space, etc., there are trade-offs. First, no matter what the advertisements say, you'll likely not get rich working in your pajamas. Top businesses decisions are still made with face-to-face meetings, handshakes, and lots of interaction. There may be a way to combine what you want to do from home, like recruiting, consulting, or selling your own products, or products you may buy at wholesale, with limited outside interaction.

Some major corporations, like Dell, American Express, Hewlett-Packard and AT&T offer work-at-home positions on an as needed basis. In order to locate at-home positions with major corporations, obtain company info from websites that post hard-to-find job postings, and a snapshot of the company's overall performance.

When applying for a work at home position, you must do your research. Avoid paying sign-up and registration fees for work from home jobs. Legitimate companies typically have enough revenue to hire you without asking for money. Expect some training, via the internet, phone, and possibly in person.

The STAR Career Workbook

In some cases, the work-from-home option may be a business you are setting up for yourself. In these cases, you will have some investment to make. Again, do your research. Check out those too-good-to-be-true deals that offer low-cost start-up, as they often have underlying costs for purchasing inventory, acquiring support, getting trained, and more.

Apprenticeships & Internships

Apprenticeship is an arrangement in which someone learns an art, trade, or job under another person. Most of the training is done on the job while working for the person, or for an employer. You may be required to continue working for this employer, for an agreed period of time, after you become skilled in the job.

An **intern** is one who works in a temporary position, with an emphasis on on-the-job training, rather than merely employment. It is similar to an apprenticeship. Interns are usually college or university students, but they can also be adults seeking skills for a new career. Internships provide opportunities to gain experience in a field, determine if you have an interest in a particular career, create a network of contacts, or gain school credit.

Internships provide the employers with cheap or free labor, for (typically) low-level tasks. An internship may be paid, unpaid, or partially paid (in the form of a stipend). Paid internships are most common in the medical, architecture science, engineering, law, business (especially accounting and finance), technology, and advertising fields.

How to find Internships

- **Company websites:** You should check with any large company, located within a reasonable distance from your university (or your home, if that is where you will be physically located during the intern period). Check company websites, and feel free to call the company human resources department, to ask if they hire interns.

- **Main technical job boards:** Many of the large job boards list intern positions. Some of my favorites for intern listings include Craigslist, DICE, and Monster. If there is a professional association site specific to your major, make sure you check there as well. Electrical engineers, for example, would want to be sure to check the listings on IEEE.org. Those candidates interested in green technology or clean technology, should check out the resources in the Green Tech and Clean Tech Job Boards. You should also check the job search engines for intern positions, such as Indeed.com. Make sure you change the search terms that you use on these. You can search for "intern" and check the results. Then go back and run a different search using different terms, such as "temporary". Play around with, and refine the terms you use, to get the most results available for your location and technical interests.

- **Niche job boards:** There are job boards that exist specifically for hiring students and graduates. Top sites include WayUp.com, InternJobs.com, Internships.com, and YouTern. LinkedIn also lists many internship opportunities.

- **Temporary Employment Agencies:** Many of the "temp" and contracting agencies have contacts at the local companies, and can help get you a part time or short-term assignment. If all else fails, and you can't find an internship within the focus of your studies, they may be able to help you get other short-term employment, that will provide experience and references for your next job search.

 **The STAR Career Workbook**

Freelancing

You can put your skills to work in many freelancing gigs while continuing your full time career search. Consider your technical, professional, or managerial skills and how they could be utilized on short assignments. Freelance gigs are offered for many of these jobs.

Freelance jobs are projects which may last just a few hours or over a few months. My personal experience is that they are very short and can be completed in the evening, quickly during the day, and even over a lunch break.

Your clients will have strong expectations for the quality of your work, so do not take jobs which require skills you are still learning. You may be asked to rework or correct items, and it will be your obligation to do this before getting paid.

In one period of my career, around the time I was writing the first version of the STAR Career Workbook, I was freelancing with Resume Writing, Career Counseling, Branding, and Marketing work. This supplemented my income, while I consulted through a major outplacement firm, independently headhunted for two high tech start-ups, and continued my search for a full time role.

Some resources to check out and sites where you can find Freelancing jobs include the following:
- upwork.com
- freelancer.com
- fiverr.com

The STAR Career Workbook

Survival Job

Randall S. Hansen, Ph.D. defined a Survival Job as *"Typically a low-end, low-paying job, that a displaced job-seeker takes on a temporary basis (often as a last resort) when unemployed, to cover basic living costs, in order to survive and avoid bankruptcy -- or worse."*

USA Today posted articles as early as 2003 discussing out of work software engineers, project managers and technical writers taking hourly positions at Home Depot, Best Buy and the like. In 2009, as I was helping a professional sport and event center hire 200 new staff for parking attendants and ushers, we were interviewing MBAs and engineers! My clients were hesitant at first, but I convinced them, that since all of their jobs were short term, and had high predictable turn-over, they should employ the best talent they could get at the time.

A Survival Job should only be a temporary, stopgap measure. You'll want to consider a Survival Job if the weekly income you can bring in from unemployment insurance does not (and it likely won't) cover your basic expenses. You'll want to consider a Survival Job after you have balanced your budget and determined when your severance pay (if any), and savings, will dip below acceptable levels. Start searching for and lining up that Survival Job well before you hit that deadline!

If you take a Survival Job, make sure you still have the flexibility to network, job search, and interview. You will not list the Survival Job on your resume, nor should anyone expect you to. If asked, you might share with a networking contact that you are working in a temporary Survival Job, to get some bills paid, and to stay off of unemployment, but it really does not need to be discussed in an interview.

Be honest with your Survival Job employer. Let them know that you are looking to continue in your chosen career path. He or she will likely be glad to have your higher level of knowledge, skills, and abilities for whatever time you are available.

The STAR Career Workbook

Volunteering

Volunteer opportunities can be found through your networking, online searches, and by simply asking to "help out". You might volunteer your time and service to acquire skills, and advance your knowledge in a particular area. This would essentially be an unpaid apprenticeship or internship.

For the experience and for the common good.

If you have the bandwidth, time, and financial resources, nothing fills the soul more than service. Volunteer opportunities can be found with many non-profit and charity organizations, and these organizations are often in desperate need of YOUR expertise: technical, financial, fundraising, engineering, architecting, planning, organizing, human resources, etc.

Resources:

- networkforgood.org/volunteer
- idealist.org
- volunteer.gov
- volunteermatch.org

Retirement Job

Are you near retirement, looking at retiring early, or considering your options to get you there? Maybe it is time for you to consider a Retirement Job. A Retirement Job is any kind of work you do after you retire from your long-term career.

Others have defined it as any **new** career path you start after age 50. The key here is "new". Clearly, age 50 is not close to retirement; I resemble that! But if you are considering a complete transition to a new career field, after age 50 or 55, perhaps you should consider a field that will take you into your retirement years.

The possibilities are as varied as the people pursuing them. A Retirement Job can be anything from working part time in a nearby store, to contracting with large companies as a consultant, to turning a hobby like gardening into a part time landscape design business, to starting a new career as a teacher.

RetirementJobs.com, for example, highlights these categories and opportunities.

OPPORTUNITIES	DREAM JOBS
Self-Employment	BMW Test Driver
Consulting	Movie Critic
Start a Business	Brew master
Buy into a Franchise	

You can see overlap here with many of the topics I've already discussed, but there are certain aspects most people are looking for, when they consider a Retirement Job.

- Opportunity to exercise a strength or passion not previously exercised in early career.
- Do less of what I did not like in my early career, and perhaps more of what I did like.
- Flexible hours and schedule so I can travel, see family, enjoy life.
- Practical role with defined function and clear goals.
- Opportunity to give something back by leading, mentoring, serving, teaching, consulting, advising, etc.

 The STAR Career Workbook

Your Life Goes On

During your job search and career transition, your life goes on, and on, and on. I've said that your job search is a full-time job, but it should not be all-consuming. The pressure is already intense enough!

Balance your Time

As with any good work-life balance strategy, make sure you are balancing your time among Family, Fun, Faith, and Fitness. Schedule time for each. If you were a beast on managing your calendar at work, continue that practice in your job search, and plug in time for work-life balance.

Equally important: reward yourself when you hit short term and milestone goals, with extra time in any area you've had to cut short to get there. For example, if you've been spending 6 nights in a row doing extra online networking, and you've landed an appointment with a key decision-maker for the following week, take off the next evening to watch a good movie.

Family

Your family can be the most important support system to sustain you during your job search, but you must put in the time and emotional engagement to keep that system healthy. Spend time with your spouse catching up. Play games with your kids, or nephews and nieces. Call your brothers, sisters, and parents.

For some of us, however, parts of our family system may not be so healthy. Your relationship with your parents or siblings may drain you of good energy, and in that case, balancing time *away* from these family

members may be the remedy. Now is not the time, with budget and time constraints, to go deep into therapy and resolve these messes. However, if you have basic, unresolved issues, like simply forgiving and forgetting a past wrong, and your gut tells you that you can pull it off, the rewards for your emotional state will be very high, and it could set the tone for a very positive career progression.

Letting go of anger and resentment can help you to keep calm, improve your health, and increase your happiness. As Proverbs 14:30 puts it, "A heart at peace gives life to the body, but envy rots the bones." And Matthew 5:9 adds, "Blessed are the peacemakers, for they will be called children of God. Even more importantly for us all, forgiving others is a key to receiving God's forgiveness for your own sins. As Matthew 6:14 says, "For if you forgive other people when they sin against you, your heavenly Father will also forgive you."

Fun

I shouldn't need to tell you how to have fun. Keep in mind to balance this pursuit with your other commitments of family, faith, and fitness. Some things that seem "fun" can be destructive. Moderation is the key. The last thing you want during a period of unemployment or job-search is a DWI, more debt than you can imagine, or the breakdown of an important relationship.

Generally, I am encouraging you to build in some diversions for your time: some simple entertainment, some time for hobbies, some time for play and some time for rest. Friends of mine talk about slipping out on a Friday during the day to see a movie. Others enjoy mountain biking, or a pint at the pub. You can plan a quick day trip to the beach, to an amusement park, or an afternoon on the lake. I also recommend using these fun activities as rewards for completing goals within your work-search plan.

# The STAR Career Workbook

Faith

I value my faith strongly and believe that it not only sustains me, but that it has the potential to benefit many people around me. God has blessed me with a wonderful family, some great talents that I can exercise in my career, and provision for all of my basic needs. I have never gone hungry, unclothed, or homeless, and I thank God every day for this provision. I pray also that God will bless me with provisions that will allow me to be generous to others. This, I believe is the simple formula you should consider for focusing on your faith during your job search:

1. Count your blessings.
2. Thank God for your life.
3. Pray for strength and provision.
4. Forgive and deepen important relationships in your life.
5. Seek ways to give of yourself.

For some of us however, faith has been a struggle. Maybe God has been allusive to you, or the faith of your parents has seemed foreign, oppressive, or backward. You may have a broken heart, or strong bitterness or anger. But what you are missing by allowing these barriers to your faith to exist, is a community of mutual believers who will love you and support you. You are missing out on healing for your soul, and your life. You are missing a guaranteed revival of your spirit, and your purpose, and a new mission, based on solid principles. Regardless of your culture, ethnic background, religious upbringing (or lack thereof), I encourage you to find (or return to) a faith that can give you these gifts.

 *The STAR Career Workbook*

Fitness

Health matters. It's not just because it's all over the news, or because your spouse is nagging you to drop some pounds. Your life matters, and you will live better, feel better, and exude a better attitude and energy, if you are healthy.

Energy = Attitude; Attitude = Energy. When you are physically fit (not necessarily running triathlons or pumping iron – just exercising regularly and eating well), you will have more energy. That energy will translate into a better attitude, and it will show up in everything you do; job search, work, family, fun, etc. That positive energy will translate into positive emotional energy, and every potential employer you will meet, wants that positive energy on his team.

The US government's recommended physical activity guidelines call for healthy adults to do at least two and a half hours of moderate intensity activity, or 75 minutes of vigorous intensity activity, every week. They also recommend you add 30 to 45 minutes of muscle-strengthening exercises at least twice a week.

All workout programs should include safety precautions, warm-up, conditioning that includes strengthening, and a cool-down. Plus, programs should progress at a safe rate for each person, and should include components of aerobic fitness, strength and resistance exercise, and flexibility.

Never have to pay for a push up. I am not advocating that you go out and join a gym, pay for a fitness boot camp, or hire a personal trainer. *Who can afford any of this during a job search?* Not only should you not stretch your budget for these services, you should not stretch your time

The STAR Career Workbook

with these activities. They can become obtrusive hobbies, as you'll read about below.

Arnold Schwarzenegger once said (imagine his Eastern European accent), "I neva haav to paay foh a poosh aup." Get out and walk or jog, do some push-ups and sit-ups, find some free aerobics classes, and create a workout plan that is right for you. A simple search on Google for "free fitness plans" resulted in over 75 million hits. I encourage you to research this for yourself, and find the sources you like.

Staying on Track

Just as I emphasize "staying on message" with your Professional Introduction, it is important that you stay on track with your career pursuits. I discussed in the chapter on Alternative Career Move Options, that many ideas will start flying by you during your career search, such as MLMs. You will also see offers to become a day trader, sell insurance, or make a career off of Youtube or Google. Lots of good people do these things, and you may try one of them, but chances are strong that you will eventually return to your career path. I just don't want that diversion to hurt your employability down the line, so I advise you to stay on track.

You have taken so much time to work through this workbook, discovering your values, strengths, career vision, accomplishment stories, network and so much more. Give this effort the full measure of your energy and commitment. Stay focused on these goals. Track your results and celebrate your successes!

The STAR Career Workbook

Time-Balancing Worksheet

Take some time now to think through some concerns you may have in balancing Family, Fun, Faith, and Fitness. List some short-term goals to make sure these important areas are balanced in your life.

Family

Concern:
Goal:

Fun

Concern:
Goal:

Faith

Concern:
Goal:

Fitness

Concern:
Goal:

The STAR Career Workbook

Taking on Hobbies

Taking on a new hobby, or escalating involvement in an existing hobby, during your job-search, can be both helpful and hurtful. Let's look at some of the basic guidance to managing a hobby and weigh the pros and cons.

A hobby should, if at all possible:	A hobby should never, especially during job search:
— Be relevant to your career path, education, and technical skills. — Connect you with other people who can further your job search. — Involve no more than 8 hours per week, preferably less, and not during prime business hours.	— Interfere with your job search, taking large amounts of time away from moving your career forward. — Interfere with the higher priorities of family, faith and fitness. — Harm, or have the potential to harm, your professional image.

HOBBY PROS:	HOBBY CONS:
— Opportunity to learn a new skill relevant to your career. — Opportunity to meet new people who can further your job search. — Opportunity to build a potential new business, either now, or later towards retirement.	— Can be physically dangerous with potential for injury, which would negatively impact your career. — Can take you off track from your career search, by providing ideas for a new business pursuit, which might not be feasible, sustainable, or profitable.

The STAR Career Workbook

The Search Goes On

Here's what I know, unfortunately. Your search may go on for a while, no matter how diligent you are at applying the strategies you have learned in this workbook.

Things to Do

1. Continue to network.

Hopefully you have taken the time to review the material on Networking, including Networking Basics, filling the Networking Funnel, and using online and social networking media. Continue to build your contact network, and penetrate target companies. Remember that your objective is to become a known quantity, so that the team will pre-select you when the next hiring opportunity arises. You will become the insider; the person you have been competing against all along and didn't know it.

Checklist:

— Re-visit Chapter 1 on the STAR networking methodology. Where have you been finding yourself, as a candidate for the opportunities you have been pursuing? Were you on the outside or inside? What do you need to do?

— Revisit the Chapter on Networking Basics in this book. Have you mapped out your various networks, and found contact information for the many people you listed? Have you contacted them yet? Get back into your networking!

— Make tools for yourself to track and work on your network. Revisit the examples of the Networking Pyramid, among others. Build your own.

 *The STAR Career Workbook*

2. Connect with, and continue to attend, meetings with support groups.

There are many possible sources for support groups you might attend. Check out local churches for programs on career search support. The Department of Labor provides resources for Workforce Centers across the country, and these centers usually provide weekly or monthly support group meetings, with trainers, networking, and job leads. Many other non-profit groups are meeting around the country, as we continue to cycle through each economic crunch. Search online for groups in your area and get connected.

Additionally, you could set up a small Career Support Group of your own. I recommend a group of around 5 to 7, but no more than 12. The extra headcount can help keep attendance up when various members can't make a meeting. Set up a weekly meeting where you can check in and support each other in your search. A Career Support Group can serve as your council of advisors. It should also help you plan, and stay on track, with your search project. It should also help you network. Various members may introduce you to contacts, who can lead you to higher level relationships, in your target companies.

Here is a possible agenda for a Career Support Group meeting:
1. Check in and see how everyone is feeling about their search.
2. Each member gives a report on his/her progress in the past week or two.
3. Each member may then report on any major breakthrough, so the team can celebrate and learn from it.
4. Finally, each member should set their priorities for the following week or two, so the group can help hold him/her accountable to those efforts.

Through the course of the Career Support Group meeting, and through the life of the group, members should remain supportive, challenging, and encouraging; offering ideas, leads, and questions.

 *The STAR Career Workbook*

3. Continue improving your marketing materials, especially your resume, forever.

Your resume and your cover letters are "living documents". You should anticipate making changes often, throughout your job search. As you transition into a new job, remember the struggle you may have had in re-constructing these marketing materials when you started this last search, and make it a part of your routine, to continuously update and manage your career marketing materials.

4. Learn from your networking meetings and interviews

I take lots of notes in my networking meetings, sales calls, interviews, etc. You probably will also. The shame of it all is when I take those notes, stick them in a file, and forget them. Make sure you go back through your notes to identify to-do items, transfer those into your calendar or task manager, and follow up on those action items.

Also, remember to build on your contacts, and continue to cultivate the relationships you open during your search. A thank you card and a quick follow up call are helpful. But you should also put a reminder on your calendar, to follow up, 3 months out, 6 months out, etc. Have another lunch or coffee and catch up, and find a way you can give them the gift of your time, service or networks.

Checklist:

— Decide which calendar or task management tool (online or paper) you will use.
— Enter notes, tasks, and reminders from your recent meetings.
— Look through the various business cards you have collected, and new contacts you have made online, and plan for time to follow up with them.

The STAR Career Workbook

5. **Plan, manage your time, and track your results.**

As you continue to search, network, interview, and search even more, remember to plan your days, weeks, and months. Manage your time, set your goals, and track your results, using some of the tools I have provided in this workbook, as well as any others you may find elsewhere.

Checklist:

— Re-visit the chapter on Networking and find the Career Search Productivity Tracker.
— Male a version of this for yourself, using Excel or any other tool that works for you.

NOTES AND ACTION ITEMS:

_____
_____
_____
_____
_____
_____
_____
_____
_____
_____
_____
_____
_____
_____
_____

 # The STAR Career Workbook

Wrapping up and moving Forward

It's time to wrap up this workbook and get you moving forward! I hope you will return to this workbook often, completing any worksheets you may have skipped, as they become more relevant to your present needs, or reading sections again, to remind you of your task at hand.

If you follow the plans, steps, and goals in this workbook, you should see a significantly reduced time on your job search, until you are re-employed, or better employed.

The "work" in this workbook **IS** the work of career planning and career search. Wash, rinse, and repeat. Keep re-evaluating, keep planning, keep networking, keep pursuing, and you will get the results you desire.

You will hear the saying that life is about the journey, and not the destination. I think this saying is wrong. You have goals, and those goals are measurable. When you get there, you will know you have succeeded... and then you'll plan for the next "there".

 **The STAR Career Workbook**

Prepare for the blessing

God reminds me to keep storing my treasures in heaven, by:

- Working as if I am working for Him -because I am. (Colossians 3:23-24)
- Learn from my successes <u>and</u> failures. (James 1: 2-4)
- Be a part of the Body of believers, using the gifts He has given me. (1 Corinthians 12)
- Give a portion of my time, talent and treasure to Him (Matthew 6:21; Luke 6:38; Romans 12:1)
- Always give Him the Glory. (Psalm 115; Colossians 3:17)

And if I do this, God says, Stand back and watch me pour out so much blessing on you that you will not have room to store it! (Proverbs 3: 9-10; Malachi 3: 10-18)

Prepare to pay it forward

So, as you fight your way forward, to find your next career goal, prepare to "pay it forward" to others who are just a little, or a lot, behind you on this journey.

<u>Checklist:</u>

- Find a mentee who needs your help and share what you have learned from me and others.
- Build on your skills and organize your personal intellectual property, so that you can make a HUGE and FAST impact for your future employer.
- Invest your time, talent, and treasures into Kingdom work, supporting missions, the sick, the poor, homeless, orphans, widows, or the elderly.

About the Author

Dan Medlin
Austin, TX
dan.medlin.starhr@gmail.com
linkedin.com/in/danmedlin
danmedlin.wordpress.com
facebook.com/AustinStarHR

Dan has 30 years of professional experience in career counseling, professional development, leadership coaching, human resources management, and global recruiting leadership. He has worked in Talent Acquisition leadership roles for global agencies including Robert Half International, and top corporations including GE, Samsung, and AMD.

In 2001, Dan incorporated LoneStar Diversified Holdings, through which he has launched a variety of staffing, headhunting, and HR consulting businesses, including in 2009, StarHR, a practice offering executive search, local, and global recruiting, HR and talent acquisition consulting and outplacement services. Through StarHR, Dan also developed the STAR Career Workshops, and this STAR Career Workbook, relying on his many years in HR, Recruiting, and Career Counseling, to document the Best Practices he has seen in job search.

Dan lives in the Austin, TX area. He is a grace-humbled Christian, blessed husband, and proud father. He is active in his church and community. Dan firmly believes in the grace of Jesus Christ, to save and lead everyone who puts their faith in Him, to an abundant life. It is by His grace, and the prompting of the Holy Spirit that this book was written originally, and revised again this year.

Dan lives with his wife and children just south of Austin, TX. They are partners with Vertical Chapel, a thriving, non-denominational Christian church. Dan serves on the Board and plays bass guitar on the Worship team. Dan's wife, Lisa leads an adoption and foster care ministry called Embrace. Dan & Lisa have 5 children (two adopted), from ages 5 to 23.

# The STAR Career Workbook

For Additional Assistance

If you are seeking additional 1:1 executive coaching, leadership advice, or career counseling, send an email, with the subject line indicating your desired service, attach your current resume, and include your contact information, to: dan.medlin.starhr@gmail.com. Someone from the team will email you back with a proposal and contract for you to accept before scheduling your first appointment.

If you are on the Job Hunt

Please note that StarHR is not in the business of "finding you a job". That is what this workbook, or our career coaching are for; to equip you to find your next career move. So, if you are sending us your resume so that we will recruit you for an open role we are filling for one of our clients, we may only follow up with you if we have a role that requires your knowledge, skills, and experience.

CPSIA information can be obtained
at www.ICGtesting.com
Printed in the USA
LVHW081101040420
652208LV00009B/813